VEGAN BAKING
COOKBOOK

Over 100 Fail-Safe recipes for vegan cakes, cookies, bread, and more, including gluten-free options

Andrew Rabbio

Table of Contents

Chapter 1: Introduction: All About Vegan Baking

The Popularity of Vegan Baking..2
Navigating the Challenges of Vegan Baking.......................2
Mastering Egg Substitutes in Vegan Baking.......................3
Mastering Gluten-Free Baking: A Simple Substitution Guide................4

Chapter 2: Muffins, Scones, Pancakes & Biscuits

Spiced Apple Bran Muffins..8
Banana Walnut Muffins..9
Maple Sweet Potato Pancakes..10
Cinnamon Rolls..11
Lemon Blueberry Pancakes...12
Buttermilk Biscuits..13
Lemon Poppyseed Muffins..14
Banana Blueberry Oat Muffins...15
Maple Chai Pumpkin Muffins..16
Dark Chocolate Cherry Scones..17
Strawberry Banana Buckwheat Pancakes...........................18
Cinnamon Sugar Donuts..19
Pecan Sticky Buns..20
Raspberry Double Chocolate Muffins...................................21
Snickerdoodle Scones..22
Orange Chocolate Chip Scones..23
Chocolate Espresso Muffins...24
Irish Cheddar Spring Onion Biscuits......................................25

Chapter 3: Cookies, Brownies, & Bars

Fudge Brownies..27
Peanut Butter Cookie Bars...28
Lemon Bars...29
Pumpkin Oatmeal Cookies...30
Carrot Cake Breakfast Cookies...31
Classic Chocolate Chip Cookies...32
Maple Pecan Bars..33
Cheesecake Brownies...34
Chocolate Cherry Brownies..35
Dark Chocolate Chambord Brownies..36
No-Bake Cookie Dough Bars..37
Chocolate Hazelnut Thumbprint Cookies..38
Sugar Cookies...39
Double Chocolate Sea Salt Cookies...40
Gingerbread Oatmeal Cream pie Cookies...41
Ginger Molasses Cookies..42
Vanilla Wafers..43
Almond Anise Biscotti..44
Red Velvet Sandwich Cookies..45
Shortbread Cookies...46
Lemon Crinkle Cookies..47
Pecan Snowball Cookies...48
Apricot Pistachio Oat Bars...49

Chapter 4: Bread

Banana Bread.. 51
Lemon Pistachio Bread..52
Pumpkin Chocolate Chip Bread..53
Jalapeño Cornbread..54
Artisan Dutch Oven Bread..55
Pumpernickel Sandwich Bread..56
Classic Sandwich Bread..57
Burger Buns..58

Sourdough Starter..59
Sourdough Bread..60
Garlic and Herb Bread..61
Ciabatta Bread..62
Orange Zucchini Bread..63
Rosemary and Garlic Focaccia Bread..64
Spinach Tomato Babka..65
Garlic Herb Naan..66
Spiced Christmas Bread..67
Butterscotch Bread Pudding...68
French Toast Bread Pudding...69
Hot Buttered Rum Bread Pudding...70

Chapter 5: Cakes & Cupcakes

Raspberry Swirl Cheesecake...72
Pumpkin Spice Sheet Cake..73
Berry Chantilly Cake...74
Black Forest Cake..75
Lemon Olive Oil Cake...76
Blueberry Bergamot Cupcakes...77
Strawberry Champagne Cupcakes..78
Apple Cinnamon Bundt Cake...79
Cinnamon Coffee Cake..80
Raspberry Coffee Cake..81
Lemon Pound Cake..82
Flourless Chocolate Cake..83
Chocolate Lava Cake..84
Pineapple Carrot Cake...85
Cherry Almond Cupcakes...86
Chocolate Beet Cake..87
Dark Chocolate Pear Cake...88
Chocolate Vermouth Cake..89

Chapter 6: Pies, Tarts, & Pastries

Vegan Pie Crust 91
Vegan Tart Crust 92
Chocolate Ganache Tart 93
Classic Pumpkin Pie 94
Fruit Tart with Vanilla Cashew Cream 95
Key Lime Pie 96
Apple Fritters 97
Banana Rum Tart 98
Mango Coconut Cream Tart 99
Coconut Panna Cotta 100
Herbed Tomato Balsamic Tart 101
Ginger Fig Tart with Coconut Crust 102
Cornflake Tart 103
Apple Frangipane Tart 104
Apple Cranberry Gingersnap Pie 105
Eggnog Custard Tart 106
Bourbon Peach Cobbler 107
Mixed Berry Cobbler 108
Vegan Apple Strudel 109
Blueberry Cream Cheese Danish 110
Brandy Pear Pie 111

© **Copyright 2023–All rights reserved**

The content contained within this book may not be reproduced, duplicated or transmitted without direct written permission from the author or the publisher. Under no circumstances will any blame or legal responsibility be held against the publisher, or author, for any damages, reparation, or monetary loss due to the information contained within this book, either directly or indirectly.

Legal Notice:

This book is copyright protected. It is only for personal use. You cannot amend, distribute, sell, use, quote or paraphrase any part, or the content within this book, without the consent of the author or publisher.

Disclaimer Notice:

Please note the information contained within this document is for educational and entertainment purposes only. All effort has been executed to present accurate, up to date, reliable, complete information. No warranties of any kind are declared or implied. Readers acknowledge that the author is not engaged in the rendering of legal, financial, medical or professional advice. The content within this book has been derived from various sources. Please consult a licensed professional before attempting any techniques outlined in this book.

By reading this document, the reader agrees that under no circumstances is the author responsible for any losses, direct or indirect, that are incurred as a result of the use of the information contained within this document, including, but not limited to, errors, omissions, or inaccuracies.

CHAPTER 1

Introduction: All About Vegan Baking

The Popularity of Vegan Baking

In a culinary landscape marked by innovation, vegan baking has swiftly transitioned from a niche choice to a widespread sensation. Recent statistics from the Plant Based Foods Association highlight double-digit growth in sales of plant-based baking essentials, surpassing industry averages. Fueled by ethical considerations, heightened health awareness, and a commitment to environmental sustainability, vegan baking resonates with a diverse audience. Its appeal is further amplified by the pervasive influence of social media, showcasing visually enticing vegan creations and extending the reach of plant-based baking to new enthusiasts.

This trend not only reflects a transformative shift in consumer preferences but also signifies a collective yearning for more sustainable, ethical, and health-conscious food choices. As industry players invest significantly in plant-based alternatives, the integration of vegan baking into everyday culinary practices becomes more seamless, underscoring its enduring influence on shaping the way we approach and enjoy delightful, plant-powered creations.

Navigating the Challenges of Vegan Baking

While the world of vegan baking is brimming with innovation, it does come with its unique set of challenges. Common pitfalls include dense textures, sunken cakes, or issues with leavening that might leave bakers feeling perplexed. Understanding these challenges and knowing how to troubleshoot them is key to mastering the art of vegan baking. Common Mistakes and Remedies:

Dense Textures: Achieving the desired lightness in vegan baked goods can be challenging. One common mistake is using too much flour or overmixing the batter. To remedy this, ensure precise measurements and avoid overmixing, which can activate gluten and lead to a denser texture. Additionally, incorporating ingredients like applesauce, vinegar, or baking powder can enhance leavening and contribute to a lighter crumb.

Sinking Cakes: Witnessing a beautifully risen cake collapse after leaving the oven can be disheartening. This may occur due to inadequate leavening or overmixing the batter. To remedy a sunken cake, ensure your leavening agents are fresh and accurately measured.

Additionally, gently fold wet and dry ingredients together, avoiding excessive mixing, to maintain the structure. Checking the oven temperature for accuracy is also crucial to guarantee even baking.

Dry or Crumbly Texture: Achieving moisture without relying on eggs or dairy can be a challenge. Overbaking or using too much flour are common culprits for a dry or crumbly texture. To combat this, monitor baking times closely and consider adding moisture-rich ingredients like mashed bananas, applesauce, or non-dairy yogurt to the batter. Adjusting the liquid-to-dry ingredient ratio can significantly enhance the final texture.

Unpleasant Aftertaste: Certain plant-based ingredients may impart unwanted flavors if not properly balanced. To avoid this, ensure that ingredients like flaxseed, baking soda, or apple cider vinegar are fresh, and use them in moderation. Opt for high-quality extracts and flavorings to enhance the taste without overpowering the baked goods.

Understanding and overcoming these challenges not only refines your baking skills but also ensures that vegan treats are as delicious and satisfying as their non-vegan counterparts. As you navigate the nuances of vegan baking, experimentation and a willingness to learn from each batch will contribute to your mastery of this art.

Mastering Egg Substitutes in Vegan Baking

Eggs are multifunctional powerhouses in traditional baking, providing structure, moisture, leavening, and emulsification. In vegan baking, finding suitable egg substitutes is crucial to replicate these functions and achieve the desired texture, structure, and flavor. Understanding the roles eggs play in baking allows us to appreciate why these substitutions are essential for successful vegan recipes.

Roles of Eggs in Baking:

- Structure: Eggs act as binders, providing structural support to baked goods. They help create a stable framework, contributing to the overall texture and form of the final product.

- Moisture: Eggs add moisture to recipes, preventing baked goods from becoming dry. This moisture content contributes to a tender and palatable texture.

- Leavening: Eggs contribute to leavening, promoting the rise of baked goods. The gases released during baking help create a light and fluffy texture.

- Emulsification: Eggs act as emulsifiers, helping fats and liquids blend seamlessly. This emulsifying role enhances the overall consistency and mouthfeel of baked goods.

Common Egg Replacements and Their Functions:

- Flax Eggs: A mixture of ground flaxseeds and water mimics the binding and moisture-retaining properties of eggs. The high omega-3 fatty acid content in flax adds a nutritional bonus.
- Chia Eggs: Similar to flax eggs, a combination of chia seeds and water creates a gel-like substance that acts as a binder and provides moisture.
- Applesauce: This fruit puree is an excellent substitute for moisture. Its natural sweetness can also enhance the flavor of baked goods. Use unsweetened applesauce for better control over sweetness levels.
- Bananas: Mashed ripe bananas not only add moisture but also contribute a natural sweetness. They work well in recipes where a subtle banana flavor complements the other ingredients.
- Silken Tofu: Blended silken tofu serves as an excellent binder and moisture contributor. Its neutral flavor makes it adaptable to a variety of recipes.
- Vinegar and Baking Soda: The chemical reaction between vinegar and baking soda produces carbon dioxide, providing leavening. This combination is particularly effective in recipes requiring a rise, such as cakes and muffins.

Understanding the functions of eggs in baking and selecting the appropriate substitute based on the desired outcome is a pivotal aspect of successful vegan baking. Each substitute brings its unique characteristics, allowing for versatility and creativity in plant-based recipes. Experimentation, coupled with an understanding of the roles these substitutes play, empowers bakers to craft delicious vegan treats with confidence and precision.

Mastering Gluten-Free Baking: A Simple Substitution Guide

In the world of baking, the art of creating gluten-free delights has become increasingly important to accommodate various dietary preferences and restrictions. For those embarking on the gluten-free journey, this cookbook not only offers an array of delicious vegan recipes but also provides a straightforward guide to adapt them to gluten-free alternatives.

Understanding Gluten-Free Baking:

Gluten, a protein found in wheat and related grains, provides the structure and elasticity crucial for traditional baked goods. In gluten-free baking, replicating this structure becomes an exciting challenge. Thankfully, with the right flour blends and a touch of experimentation, creating gluten-free versions of your favorite recipes is both achievable and delectable.

Simple Substitution Guide:

For recipes that can be easily adapted to be gluten-free, we've included a straightforward substitution guide at the bottom of each page. This guide suggests alternative gluten-free flours or blends to replace traditional wheat flour. Keep in mind that not all gluten-free flour blends are created equal, and individual preferences may vary. If your first attempt doesn't yield the desired result, don't be discouraged—consider trying a different gluten-free flour blend to suit your taste and texture preferences.

Preferred Gluten-Free Flour Blends:

While various gluten-free flour blends exist, I personally recommend Bob's Red Mill 1:1 Gluten-Free Baking Flour for its versatility and reliable results in many recipes. Additionally, King Arthur Gluten-Free All-Purpose Flour and Cup4Cup have proven to be excellent alternatives, each with its unique characteristics that contribute to successful gluten-free baking.

Exploring More Gluten-Free Delights: Discover "The Simple Art of Gluten-Free Baking Cookbook"

If you find joy in the world of gluten-free baking and wish to delve deeper into a myriad of delectable recipes, consider exploring my dedicated cookbook, "The Simple Art of Gluten-Free Baking." This comprehensive collection is brimming with a diverse array of gluten-free treats that cater to various tastes and preferences. Inside, you'll discover a treasure trove of recipes designed with the gluten-sensitive in mind. What's more, many of these recipes offer easy substitutions to make them entirely vegan, ensuring a delightful experience for those embracing plant-based living.

"The Simple Art of Gluten-Free Baking Cookbook" invites you to embark on a culinary adventure where the absence of gluten doesn't compromise on flavor, texture, or creativity. Unleash your passion for gluten-free and vegan delights, exploring a world of possibilities that redefine the art of baking for all dietary preferences.

CHAPTER 2

Muffins, Scones, Pancakes & Biscuits

Spiced Apple Bran Muffins

Ingredients:

- 1 1/2 cups (180g) all-purpose flour
- 1/2 cup (60g) wheat bran
- 1 teaspoon (5g) baking powder
- 1/2 teaspoon (3g) baking soda
- 1/2 teaspoon (3g) salt
- 1 teaspoon (3g) ground cinnamon
- 1/2 teaspoon (1g) ground nutmeg
- 1/4 teaspoon (1g) ground ginger
- 1/4 cup (60ml) vegetable oil
- 1/2 cup (120ml) unsweetened applesauce
- 1/2 cup (120ml) maple syrup or agave nectar
- 1/4 cup (60ml) plant-based milk (such as almond, soy, or oat)
- 1 teaspoon (5ml) vanilla extract
- 1 cup (150g) grated apple
- 1/2 cup (60g) chopped walnuts or pecans (optional)

Directions:

1. Preheat your oven to 350°F (175°C) and line a muffin tin with paper liners.
2. In a large mixing bowl, whisk together the all-purpose flour, wheat bran, baking powder, baking soda, salt, cinnamon, nutmeg, and ginger.
3. In a separate bowl, combine the vegetable oil, applesauce, maple syrup or agave nectar, plant-based milk, and vanilla extract. Mix well.
4. Pour the wet ingredients into the dry ingredients and stir until just combined. Be careful not to overmix; a few lumps are okay.
5. Fold in the grated apple and chopped nuts (if using).
6. Spoon the batter into the muffin cups, filling each about 2/3 full.
7. Bake in the preheated oven for 18-22 minutes or until a toothpick inserted into the center of a muffin comes out clean.
8. Allow the muffins to cool in the tin for 5 minutes, then transfer them to a wire rack to cool completely.

Gluten-Free Option:

- Substitute all-purpose flour and wheat bran with a gluten-free 1:1 flour blend.
- Add 1/2 teaspoon xanthan gum to the dry ingredients if the 1:1 flour doesn't have xanthan gum included.
- Ensure that the baking powder and baking soda are also gluten-free.

Banana Walnut Muffins

Ingredients:

- 1 1/2 cups (180g) all-purpose flour
- 1/2 cup (60g) oat flour
- 1 teaspoon (5g) baking powder
- 1/2 teaspoon (3g) baking soda
- 1/4 teaspoon (1g) salt
- 1/2 teaspoon (2g) ground cinnamon
- 1/4 cup (60ml) coconut oil, melted
- 1/2 cup (120ml) maple syrup or agave nectar
- 1/4 cup (60ml) plant-based milk (such as almond, soy, or oat)
- 1 teaspoon (5ml) vanilla extract
- 3 ripe bananas, mashed
- 1/2 cup (60g) chopped walnuts

Directions:

1. Preheat your oven to 350°F (175°C) and line a muffin tin with paper liners.
2. In a large mixing bowl, whisk together the all-purpose flour, oat flour, baking powder, baking soda, salt, and ground cinnamon.
3. In a separate bowl, mix together the melted coconut oil, maple syrup or agave nectar, plant-based milk, and vanilla extract.
4. Add the wet ingredients to the dry ingredients and stir until just combined.
5. Fold in the mashed bananas and chopped walnuts.
6. Spoon the batter into the muffin cups, filling each about 2/3 full.
7. Bake in the preheated oven for 18-22 minutes or until a toothpick inserted into the center of a muffin comes out clean.
8. Allow the muffins to cool in the tin for 5 minutes, then transfer them to a wire rack to cool completely.

Gluten-Free Option:

- Substitute all-purpose flour with a gluten-free 1:1 flour blend.
- Add 1/2 teaspoon xanthan gum to the dry ingredients if the 1:1 flour doesn't have xanthan gum included.
- Ensure that the baking powder and baking soda are also gluten-free.

Maple Sweet Potato Pancakes

Yield: Approximately 8 pancakes

Ingredients:

- 1 cup (120g) all-purpose flour
- 1 tablespoon (14g) baking powder
- 1/2 teaspoon (2g) cinnamon
- 1/4 teaspoon (1g) nutmeg
- 1/4 teaspoon (1g) salt
- 1 cup (240g) mashed sweet potato (cooked and cooled or canned)
- 1 cup (240ml) plant-based milk (such as almond, soy, or oat)
- 3 tablespoons (45g) maple syrup
- 2 tablespoons (27g) vegetable oil
- 1 teaspoon (5g) vanilla extract
- Optional add-ins:
- 1/4 cup (30g) chopped pecans or walnuts
- 1/4 cup (40g) raisins or dried cranberries

Directions:

1. In a large mixing bowl, whisk together the all-purpose flour, baking powder, cinnamon, nutmeg, and salt.
2. In a separate bowl, whisk together the mashed sweet potato, plant-based milk, maple syrup, vegetable oil, and vanilla extract until well combined.
3. Pour the wet ingredients into the dry ingredients and stir until just combined. If using, fold in the optional add-ins.
4. Heat a griddle or non-stick skillet over medium heat. Lightly grease with cooking spray or a small amount of vegetable oil.
5. Pour 1/4 cup of batter onto the griddle for each pancake, spreading it slightly with the back of a spoon.
6. Cook until bubbles form on the surface of the pancake and the edges look set, then flip and cook the other side until golden brown.
7. Repeat until all the batter is used, adjusting the heat as needed to prevent burning.
8. Serve the pancakes warm with your favorite toppings, such as maple syrup, sliced bananas, or a dollop of vegan whipped cream.

Gluten-Free Option:

- Substitute all-purpose flour with a gluten-free 1:1 flour blend.
- Add 1/4 teaspoon xanthan gum to the dry ingredients if the 1:1 flour doesn't have xanthan gum included.
- Ensure that the baking powder is also gluten-free.

Cinnamon Rolls

Yield: 12 cinnamon rolls

Ingredients:

- Dough Ingredients:
- 1 cup (240ml) plant-based milk (such as almond, soy, or oat)
- 1/4 cup (60g) vegan butter, melted
- 1/4 cup (50g) granulated sugar
- 2 1/4 teaspoons (7g) active dry yeast
- 3 1/2 cups (420g) all-purpose flour
- 1/2 teaspoon (3g) salt
- Filling Ingredients:
- 1/2 cup (100g) brown sugar, packed
- 2 tablespoons (16g) ground cinnamon
- 1/4 cup (60g) vegan butter, softened
- Frosting Ingredients:
- 1 cup (120g) powdered sugar
- 2 tablespoons (30ml) plant-based milk
- 1/2 teaspoon vanilla extract

Directions:

1. Dough: Warm the plant-based milk in a saucepan or microwave until it's lukewarm (around 110°F or 43°C).
2. In a large mixing bowl, combine the warm plant-based milk, melted vegan butter, and granulated sugar. Sprinkle the yeast on top and let it sit for about 5 minutes until foamy.
3. Add the flour and salt to the yeast mixture. Mix until a dough forms.
4. Knead the dough on a floured surface for about 5 minutes, or until it becomes smooth and elastic.
5. Place the dough in a greased bowl, cover with a damp cloth, and let it rise in a warm place for 1-1.5 hours, or until doubled in size.
6. Filling: In a small bowl, mix together the brown sugar and ground cinnamon.
7. Assembly: Preheat the oven to 350°F (175°C).
8. Roll out the dough on a floured surface into a rectangle (about 16x10 inches).
9. Spread the softened vegan butter over the surface of the dough, then evenly sprinkle the cinnamon sugar mixture.
10. Starting from the long edge, tightly roll the dough into a log.
11. Cut the log into 12 equal slices.
12. Place the slices in a greased baking dish, leaving a little space between each.
13. Bake for 25-30 minutes or until the rolls are golden brown.
14. Frosting: In a small bowl, whisk together the powdered sugar, plant-based milk, and vanilla extract until smooth.
15. Once the cinnamon rolls are out of the oven, drizzle the frosting over them while they're still warm.
16. Allow the cinnamon rolls to cool slightly before serving.

Gluten-Free Option:

- Substitute all-purpose flour with a gluten-free 1:1 flour blend.
- Add 1 1/4 teaspoons xanthan gum to the dry ingredients if the 1:1 flour doesn't have xanthan gum included.
- Ensure that the baking powder and baking soda are also gluten-free.
- To help roll the cinnamon rolls, place the dough onto a sheet of parchment before you roll the dough out. After you have spread the filling use the parchment paper to assist in rolling the dough.

Lemon Blueberry Pancakes

Yield: Approximately 8 pancakes

Ingredients:

- 1 cup (240ml) plant-based milk
- 1 tablespoon (15ml) lemon juice
- 1 tablespoon (6g) lemon zest
- 2 tablespoons (30ml) vegetable oil
- 2 tablespoons (30ml) maple syrup
- 1 cup (120g) all-purpose flour
- 1 tablespoon (15g) baking powder
- 1/2 teaspoon (3g) baking soda
- 1/4 teaspoon (1g) salt
- 1 cup (150g) fresh or frozen blueberries
- Optional Toppings:
- Additional blueberries
- Maple syrup
- Vegan butter
- Sliced bananas

Directions:

1. In a bowl, mix the plant-based milk with lemon juice and let it sit for a few minutes to create a vegan "buttermilk."
2. Add the lemon zest, vegetable oil, and maple syrup to the "buttermilk" and whisk until well combined.
3. In a separate bowl, whisk together the all-purpose flour, baking powder, baking soda, and salt.
4. Pour the wet ingredients into the dry ingredients and stir until just combined. It's okay if there are a few lumps.
5. Gently fold in the blueberries.
6. Heat a griddle or non-stick skillet over medium heat. Lightly grease with cooking spray or a small amount of vegetable oil.
7. Pour 1/4 cup of batter onto the griddle for each pancake, spreading it slightly with the back of a spoon.
8. Cook until bubbles form on the surface of the pancake and the edges look set, then flip and cook the other side until golden brown.
9. Repeat until all the batter is used, adjusting the heat as needed to prevent burning.
10. Serve the pancakes warm with your favorite toppings, such as additional blueberries, maple syrup, vegan butter, or sliced bananas.

Gluten-Free Option:

- Substitute all-purpose flour with a gluten-free 1:1 flour blend.
- Add 1/4 teaspoon xanthan gum to the dry ingredients if the 1:1 flour doesn't have xanthan gum included.
- Ensure that the baking powder and baking soda are also gluten-free.

Buttermilk Biscuits

Yield: Approximately 12 biscuits

Ingredients:

- 2 cups (480ml) plant-based milk (unsweetened)
- 1 tablespoon (15ml) apple cider vinegar
- 4 cups (480g) all-purpose flour
- 1 tablespoon (15g) baking powder
- 1 teaspoon (5g) salt
- 1/2 cup (120g) vegan butter, cold and cubed
- Additional flour for dusting

Directions:

1. Preheat the oven to 450°F (230°C). Line a baking sheet with parchment paper.
2. In a small bowl, combine the plant-based milk and apple cider vinegar. Let it sit for about 5 minutes to create a vegan "buttermilk."
3. In a large mixing bowl, whisk together the all-purpose flour, baking powder, and salt.
4. Add the cold, cubed vegan butter to the flour mixture. Using a pastry cutter or a fork, cut the butter into the flour until the mixture resembles coarse crumbs.
5. Make a well in the center of the mixture and pour in the vegan "buttermilk." Stir until just combined; do not overmix.
6. Turn the dough out onto a floured surface. Gently fold it over onto itself a few times, then pat it into a 1-inch thick rectangle.
7. Using a floured biscuit cutter or a glass, cut out biscuits and place them on the prepared baking sheet.
8. Gather any remaining dough, gently pat it down, and cut out more biscuits.
9. Bake in the preheated oven for 12-15 minutes or until the biscuits are golden brown on top.
10. Allow the biscuits to cool on the baking sheet for a few minutes before transferring them to a wire rack.
11. Serve warm with vegan butter, jam, or your favorite toppings.

Gluten-Free Option:

- Substitute all-purpose flour with a gluten-free 1:1 flour blend.
- Add 1 1/2 teaspoon xanthan gum to the dry ingredients if the 1:1 flour doesn't have xanthan gum included.
- Ensure that the baking powder is also gluten-free.

Note:

Handle the dough as little as possible for the best results, especially when making gluten-free biscuits.

Lemon Poppyseed Muffins

Yield: 12 muffins

Ingredients:

- 2 cups (240g) all-purpose flour
- 1/2 cup (100g) granulated sugar
- 1/4 cup (60ml) maple syrup or agave nectar
- 1 tablespoon (15ml) baking powder
- 1/2 teaspoon (2.5g) baking soda
- 1/4 teaspoon (1.25g) salt
- 1 cup (240ml) plant-based milk (such as almond, soy, or oat)
- 1/3 cup (80ml) vegetable oil
- Zest of 2 lemons
- 3 tablespoons (45ml) fresh lemon juice
- 1 tablespoon (10g) poppy seeds
- Glaze Ingredients:
- 1 cup (120g) powdered sugar
- 2 tablespoons (30ml) fresh lemon juice

Gluten-Free Option:

- Substitute all-purpose flour with a gluten-free 1:1 flour blend.
- Add 1/2 teaspoon xanthan gum to the dry ingredients if the 1:1 flour doesn't have xanthan gum included.
- Ensure that the baking powder and baking soda are also gluten-free.

Directions:

1. Preheat the oven to 375°F (190°C). Line a muffin tin with paper liners.
2. In a large mixing bowl, whisk together the all-purpose flour, granulated sugar, baking powder, baking soda, and salt.
3. In a separate bowl, combine the plant-based milk, vegetable oil, maple syrup or agave nectar, lemon zest, and fresh lemon juice.
4. Pour the wet ingredients into the dry ingredients and stir until just combined. Do not overmix.
5. Gently fold in the poppy seeds.
6. Spoon the batter into the muffin cups, filling each about 2/3 full.
7. Bake in the preheated oven for 18-22 minutes or until a toothpick inserted into the center of a muffin comes out clean.
8. While the muffins are baking, prepare the glaze by whisking together the powdered sugar and fresh lemon juice until smooth.
9. Once the muffins are done baking, allow them to cool in the tin for 5 minutes, then transfer them to a wire rack.
10. Drizzle the lemon glaze over the warm muffins.
11. Let the muffins cool completely before serving.

Banana Blueberry Oat Muffins

Yield: 12 muffins

Ingredients:

- 1 1/2 cups (180g) all-purpose flour
- 1/2 cup (50g) rolled oats
- 1 teaspoon (5g) baking powder
- 1/2 teaspoon (2.5g) baking soda
- 1/4 teaspoon (1.25g) salt
- 1/2 teaspoon (2g) ground cinnamon
- 3 ripe bananas, mashed
- 1/2 cup (120ml) maple syrup or agave nectar
- 1/4 cup (60ml) vegetable oil
- 1 teaspoon (5ml) vanilla extract
- 1 cup (150g) blueberries (fresh or frozen)
- Optional Topping:
- 2 tablespoons (20g) rolled oats

Directions:

1. Preheat the oven to 375°F (190°C). Line a muffin tin with paper liners.
2. In a large mixing bowl, combine the all-purpose flour, rolled oats, baking powder, baking soda, salt, and ground cinnamon.
3. In a separate bowl, mash the ripe bananas and add the maple syrup or agave nectar, vegetable oil, and vanilla extract. Mix well.
4. Pour the wet ingredients into the dry ingredients and stir until just combined.
5. Gently fold in the blueberries.
6. Spoon the batter into the muffin cups, filling each about 2/3 full.
7. If desired, sprinkle a few rolled oats on top of each muffin for a textured topping.
8. Bake in the preheated oven for 18-22 minutes or until a toothpick inserted into the center of a muffin comes out clean.
9. Allow the muffins to cool in the tin for 5 minutes, then transfer them to a wire rack.

Gluten-Free Option:

- Substitute all-purpose flour with a gluten-free 1:1 flour blend.
- Substitute rolled oats for gluten-free rolled oats
- Add 1/4 teaspoon xanthan gum to the dry ingredients if the 1:1 flour doesn't have xanthan gum included.
- Ensure that the baking powder and baking soda are also gluten-free.

Maple Chai Pumpkin Muffins

Yield: 12 muffins

Ingredients:

- 1 3/4 cups (220g) all-purpose flour
- 1 teaspoon (5g) baking powder
- 1/2 teaspoon (2.5g) baking soda
- 1/4 teaspoon (1.25g) salt
- 1 teaspoon (2g) chai spice blend (cinnamon, cardamom, ginger, cloves, and nutmeg)
- 1 cup (240g) canned pumpkin puree
- 1/2 cup (120ml) maple syrup
- 1/4 cup (60ml) vegetable oil
- 1/4 cup (60ml) plant-based milk (such as almond, soy, or oat)
- 1 teaspoon (5ml) vanilla extract
- 1/2 cup (120ml) strong brewed chai tea, cooled
- Optional Topping:
- Maple glaze (1/2 cup powdered sugar mixed with 2 tablespoons maple syrup)

Directions:

1. Preheat the oven to 375°F (190°C). Line a muffin tin with paper liners.
2. In a large mixing bowl, whisk together the all-purpose flour, baking powder, baking soda, salt, and chai spice blend.
3. In a separate bowl, combine the pumpkin puree, maple syrup, vegetable oil, plant-based milk, vanilla extract, and brewed chai tea. Mix well.
4. Pour the wet ingredients into the dry ingredients and stir until just combined.
5. Spoon the batter into the muffin cups, filling each about 2/3 full.
6. Bake in the preheated oven for 18-22 minutes or until a toothpick inserted into the center of a muffin comes out clean.
7. Allow the muffins to cool in the tin for 5 minutes, then transfer them to a wire rack.
8. If desired, drizzle the maple glaze over the cooled muffins.

Gluten-Free Option:

- Substitute all-purpose flour with a gluten-free 1:1 flour blend.
- Add 1/2 teaspoon xanthan gum to the dry ingredients if the 1:1 flour doesn't have xanthan gum included.
- Ensure that the baking powder and baking soda are also gluten-free.

Dark Chocolate Cherry Scones

Yield: 8 scones

Ingredients:

- 2 cups (240g) all-purpose flour
- 1/4 cup (50g) granulated sugar
- 1 tablespoon (12g) baking powder
- 1/2 teaspoon (2.5g) salt
- 1/2 cup (120g) vegan butter, cold and cubed
- 1/2 cup (120ml) canned coconut milk (full fat), chilled
- 1 teaspoon (5ml) vanilla extract
- 1/2 cup (90g) vegan dark chocolate chips or chunks
- 1/2 cup (75g) dried cherries, chopped
- Optional Glaze:
- 1/2 cup (60g) powdered sugar
- 1-2 tablespoons (15-30ml) plant-based milk
- 1/4 teaspoon vanilla extract

Directions:

1. Preheat the oven to 400°F (200°C). Line a baking sheet with parchment paper.
2. In a large mixing bowl, whisk together the all-purpose flour, sugar, baking powder, and salt.
3. Add the cold, cubed vegan butter to the flour mixture. Using a pastry cutter or your hands, cut the butter into the flour until the mixture resembles coarse crumbs.
4. In a separate bowl, mix the chilled coconut milk and vanilla extract.
5. Make a well in the center of the dry ingredients and pour in the coconut milk mixture. Stir until just combined.
6. Gently fold in the dark chocolate chips or chunks and the dried cherries.
7. Turn the dough out onto a floured surface. Gently pat it into a 3/4-inch thick circle.
8. Cut the circle into 8 wedges and place them on the prepared baking sheet.
9. Bake in the preheated oven for 15-18 minutes or until the scones are golden brown.
10. While the scones are baking, prepare the optional glaze by whisking together the powdered sugar, plant-based milk, and vanilla extract until smooth.
11. Once the scones are done baking, allow them to cool on the baking sheet for a few minutes before transferring them to a wire rack.
12. Drizzle the glaze over the cooled scones, if desired.

Gluten-Free Option:

- Substitute all-purpose flour with a gluten-free 1:1 flour blend.
- Add 1/2 teaspoon xanthan gum to the dry ingredients if the 1:1 flour doesn't have xanthan gum included.
- Ensure that the baking powder is also gluten-free.

Strawberry Banana Buckwheat Pancakes

Yield: Approximately 8 pancakes

Ingredients:

- 1 cup (120g) buckwheat flour
- 1/2 cup (60g) all-purpose flour
- 1 tablespoon (12g) baking powder
- 1/2 teaspoon (3g) baking soda
- 1/4 teaspoon (1g) salt
- 1 cup (240ml) plant-based milk (such as almond, soy, or oat)
- 1 ripe banana, mashed
- 1/2 cup (75g) fresh strawberries, diced
- 2 tablespoons (30ml) maple syrup
- 1 tablespoon (15ml) vegetable oil
- 1 teaspoon (5ml) vanilla extract
- Optional Toppings:
- Sliced strawberries
- Sliced bananas
- Maple syrup

Directions:

1. In a large mixing bowl, whisk together the buckwheat flour, all-purpose flour, baking powder, baking soda, and salt.
2. In a separate bowl, combine the plant-based milk, mashed banana, diced strawberries, maple syrup, vegetable oil, and vanilla extract. Mix well.
3. Pour the wet ingredients into the dry ingredients and stir until just combined. If the batter is too thick, you can add a little more plant-based milk.
4. Heat a griddle or non-stick skillet over medium heat. Lightly grease with cooking spray or a small amount of vegetable oil.
5. Pour 1/4 cup of batter onto the griddle for each pancake, spreading it slightly with the back of a spoon.
6. Cook until bubbles form on the surface of the pancake and the edges look set, then flip and cook the other side until golden brown.
7. Repeat until all the batter is used, adjusting the heat as needed to prevent burning.
8. Serve the pancakes warm with sliced strawberries, sliced bananas, and a drizzle of maple syrup.

Gluten-Free Option:

- Substitute all-purpose flour with a gluten-free 1:1 flour blend.
- Add 1/4 teaspoon xanthan gum to the dry ingredients if the 1:1 flour doesn't have xanthan gum included.
- Ensure that the baking powder and baking soda are also gluten-free.

Cinnamon Sugar Donuts

Yield: Approximately 12 donuts

Ingredients:

- For the Donuts:
- 2 cups (240g) all-purpose flour
- 3/4 cup (150g) granulated sugar
- 2 teaspoons (8g) baking powder
- 1/2 teaspoon (2.5g) baking soda
- 1/2 teaspoon (2.5g) salt
- 1 teaspoon (2g) ground cinnamon
- 1 cup (240ml) plant-based milk (such as almond, soy, or oat)
- 1/4 cup (60ml) vegetable oil
- 2 teaspoons (10ml) apple cider vinegar
- 1 teaspoon (5ml) vanilla extract
- For the Cinnamon Sugar Coating:
- 1/2 cup (100g) granulated sugar
- 1 tablespoon (12g) ground cinnamon
- 1/4 cup (60g) vegan butter, melted

Gluten-Free Option:

- Substitute all-purpose flour with a gluten-free 1:1 flour blend.
- Add 1/2 teaspoon xanthan gum to the dry ingredients if the 1:1 flour doesn't have xanthan gum included.
- Ensure that the baking powder and baking soda are also gluten-free.

Note:

- If you don't have a donut pan, you can also shape the dough into small rounds and bake them on a lined baking sheet.

Directions:

1. Preheat the oven to 375°F (190°C). Grease a donut pan with cooking spray or a small amount of vegetable oil.
2. In a large mixing bowl, whisk together the all-purpose flour, sugar, baking powder, baking soda, salt, and ground cinnamon.
3. In a separate bowl, combine the plant-based milk, vegetable oil, apple cider vinegar, and vanilla extract. Mix well.
4. Pour the wet ingredients into the dry ingredients and stir until just combined. Be careful not to overmix.
5. Spoon the batter into a piping bag or a Ziploc bag with the corner snipped off. Pipe the batter into the prepared donut pan, filling each cavity about 2/3 full.
6. Bake in the preheated oven for 12-15 minutes or until a toothpick inserted into a donut comes out clean.
7. While the donuts are baking, mix the granulated sugar and ground cinnamon for the coating in a shallow bowl.
8. Once the donuts are done, let them cool for a few minutes, then transfer them to a wire rack.
9. Brush each donut with melted vegan butter, then roll in the cinnamon sugar mixture to coat evenly.
10. Serve the donuts warm and enjoy!

Pecan Sticky Buns

Yield: Approximately 12 pecan sticky buns

Ingredients:

- For the Dough:
- 3 1/2 cups (420g) all-purpose flour
- 1/4 cup (50g) granulated sugar
- 1 packet (2 1/4 teaspoons or 7g) active dry yeast
- 1 teaspoon (5g) salt
- 1 1/4 cups (300ml) plant-based milk (such as almond, soy, or oat), warmed
- 1/4 cup (60g) vegan butter, melted
- 1 teaspoon (5ml) vanilla extract
- For the Filling:
- 1/2 cup (100g) brown sugar, packed
- 1 tablespoon (12g) ground cinnamon
- 1/4 cup (60g) vegan butter, softened
- 1 cup (120g) chopped pecans
- For the Sticky Glaze:
- 1/2 cup (115g) vegan butter
- 1 cup (200g) brown sugar, packed
- 1/4 cup (60ml) maple syrup
- 1 cup (120g) chopped pecans

Directions:

1. For the Dough: In a small bowl, combine the warmed plant-based milk and sugar. Stir until the sugar is dissolved, then add the yeast. Let it sit for 5-10 minutes until it becomes frothy.
2. In a large mixing bowl, combine the flour and salt. Make a well in the center and pour in the yeast mixture, melted vegan butter, and vanilla extract.
3. Mix until a dough forms, then knead on a floured surface for about 5-7 minutes until it becomes smooth and elastic.
4. Place the dough in a greased bowl, cover with a damp cloth, and let it rise in a warm place for 1-1.5 hours, or until doubled in size.
5. For the Filling: In a small bowl, mix together the brown sugar and ground cinnamon.
6. For the Sticky Glaze: In a saucepan, melt the vegan butter. Add the brown sugar and maple syrup, stirring until the sugar is dissolved. Remove from heat.
7. Pour the sticky glaze into the bottom of a greased baking dish. Sprinkle the chopped pecans evenly over the glaze.
8. Assembly: Punch down the risen dough and roll it out on a floured surface into a rectangle (about 16x10 inches).
9. Spread the softened vegan butter over the surface of the dough, then evenly sprinkle the brown sugar and cinnamon mixture and chopped pecans.
10. Starting from the long edge, tightly roll the dough into a log. Cut the log into 12 equal slices.
11. Place the slices in the prepared baking dish, on top of the sticky glaze.
12. Preheat the oven to 350°F (175°C) and let the buns rise for an additional 20-30 minutes while the oven is heating.
13. Bake in the preheated oven for 25-30 minutes or until the buns are golden brown.
14. Allow the buns to cool in the dish for 5 minutes, then invert onto a serving platter.
15. Serve warm and enjoy your delightful Vegan Pecan Sticky Buns!

Gluten-Free Option:

- Substitute all-purpose flour with a gluten-free 1:1 flour blend.
- Add 1 teaspoon xanthan gum to the dry ingredients if the 1:1 flour doesn't have xanthan gum included.

Raspberry Double Chocolate Muffins

Yield: Approximately 12 muffins

Ingredients:

- 1 cup (240ml) plant-based milk (such as almond, soy, or oat)
- 1 tablespoon (15ml) apple cider vinegar
- 1 3/4 cups (210g) all-purpose flour
- 1/2 cup (50g) cocoa powder
- 1 teaspoon (5g) baking powder
- 1/2 teaspoon (2.5g) baking soda
- 1/4 teaspoon (1.25g) salt
- 1/2 cup (120ml) vegetable oil
- 1 cup (200g) granulated sugar
- 1 teaspoon (5ml) vanilla extract
- 1 cup (150g) vegan chocolate chips
- 1 cup (150g) fresh or frozen raspberries

Directions:

1. Preheat the oven to 350°F (175°C). Line a muffin tin with paper liners.
2. In a measuring cup, combine the plant-based milk and apple cider vinegar. Let it sit for about 5 minutes to create a vegan "buttermilk."
3. In a large mixing bowl, whisk together the all-purpose flour, cocoa powder, baking powder, baking soda, and salt.
4. In a separate bowl, whisk together the vegetable oil, granulated sugar, and vanilla extract. Add the "buttermilk" mixture and mix until well combined.
5. Pour the wet ingredients into the dry ingredients and stir until just combined. Do not overmix.
6. Gently fold in the vegan chocolate chips and raspberries.
7. Spoon the batter into the muffin cups, filling each about 2/3 full.
8. Bake in the preheated oven for 18-22 minutes or until a toothpick inserted into the center of a muffin comes out clean.
9. Allow the muffins to cool in the tin for 5 minutes, then transfer them to a wire rack to cool completely.
10. Serve and enjoy these luscious Vegan Double Chocolate Raspberry Muffins!

Gluten-Free Option:

- Substitute all-purpose flour with a gluten-free 1:1 flour blend.
- Add 1/2 teaspoon xanthan gum to the dry ingredients if the 1:1 flour doesn't have xanthan gum included.
- Ensure that the baking powder and baking soda are also gluten-free.

Snickerdoodle Scones

Yield: 8 scones

Ingredients:

- For the Scones:
- 2 cups (240g) all-purpose flour
- 1/3 cup (67g) granulated sugar
- 1 tablespoon (15g) baking powder
- 1/2 teaspoon (2.5g) salt
- 1/2 cup (120g) vegan butter, cold and cubed
- 1/2 cup (120ml) plant-based milk (such as almond, soy, or oat)
- 1 teaspoon (5ml) vanilla extract
- For the Cinnamon Sugar Topping:
- 2 tablespoons (25g) granulated sugar
- 1 teaspoon (2g) ground cinnamon
- For the Glaze:
- 1 cup (120g) powdered sugar
- 2 tablespoons (30ml) plant-based milk
- 1/2 teaspoon (2.5ml) vanilla extract

Directions:

1. Preheat the oven to 400°F (200°C). Line a baking sheet with parchment paper.
2. In a large mixing bowl, whisk together the all-purpose flour, sugar, baking powder, and salt.
3. Add the cold, cubed vegan butter to the flour mixture. Using a pastry cutter or your hands, cut the butter into the flour until the mixture resembles coarse crumbs.
4. In a separate bowl, mix together the plant-based milk and vanilla extract.
5. Make a well in the center of the dry ingredients and pour in the wet ingredients. Stir until just combined; do not overmix.
6. Turn the dough out onto a floured surface. Gently fold it over onto itself a few times, then pat it into a 3/4-inch thick circle.
7. In a small bowl, mix together the granulated sugar and ground cinnamon for the topping.
8. Cut the dough into 8 wedges and place them on the prepared baking sheet.
9. Sprinkle the cinnamon sugar mixture over the tops of the scones.
10. Bake in the preheated oven for 12-15 minutes or until the scones are golden brown.
11. While the scones are baking, prepare the glaze by whisking together the powdered sugar, plant-based milk, and vanilla extract until smooth.
12. Once the scones are done baking, allow them to cool on the baking sheet for a few minutes before transferring them to a wire rack.
13. Drizzle the glaze over the cooled scones.
14. Serve and enjoy your Vegan Snickerdoodle Scones with a cup of your favorite plant-based milk or tea!

Gluten-Free Option:

- Substitute all-purpose flour with a gluten-free 1:1 flour blend.
- Add 3/4 teaspoon xanthan gum to the dry ingredients if the 1:1 flour doesn't have xanthan gum included.
- Ensure that the baking powder is also gluten-free.

Orange Chocolate Chip Scones

Yield: 8 scones

Ingredients:

- For the Scones:
- 2 cups (240g) all-purpose flour
- 1/3 cup (67g) granulated sugar
- 1 tablespoon (15g) baking powder
- 1/2 teaspoon (2.5g) salt
- Zest of 1 orange
- 1/2 cup (120g) vegan butter, cold and cubed
- 1/2 cup (120ml) orange juice
- 1 teaspoon (5ml) vanilla extract
- 1/2 cup (90g) vegan chocolate chips
- For the Glaze:
- 1 cup (120g) powdered sugar
- 2 tablespoons (30ml) orange juice
- Zest of 1 orange

Gluten-Free Option:

- Substitute all-purpose flour with a gluten-free 1:1 flour blend.
- Add 3/4 teaspoon xanthan gum to the dry ingredients if the 1:1 flour doesn't have xanthan gum included.
- Ensure that the baking powder is also gluten-free.

Note:

For the best texture, handle the dough as little as possible to keep the scones light and flaky.

Directions:

1. Preheat the oven to 400°F (200°C). Line a baking sheet with parchment paper.
2. In a large mixing bowl, whisk together the all-purpose flour, sugar, baking powder, salt, and orange zest.
3. Add the cold, cubed vegan butter to the flour mixture. Using a pastry cutter or your hands, cut the butter into the flour until the mixture resembles coarse crumbs.
4. In a measuring cup, combine the fresh orange juice and vanilla extract.
5. Make a well in the center of the dry ingredients and pour in the orange juice mixture. Stir until just combined; do not overmix.
6. Gently fold in the vegan chocolate chips.
7. Turn the dough out onto a floured surface. Gently fold it over onto itself a few times, then pat it into a 3/4-inch thick circle.
8. Cut the dough into 8 wedges and place them on the prepared baking sheet.
9. Bake in the preheated oven for 12-15 minutes or until the scones are golden brown.
10. While the scones are baking, prepare the glaze by whisking together the powdered sugar, fresh orange juice, and orange zest until smooth.
11. Once the scones are done baking, allow them to cool on the baking sheet for a few minutes before transferring them to a wire rack.
12. Drizzle the orange glaze over the cooled scones.
13. Serve and enjoy your Vegan Orange Chocolate Chip Scones with a cup of tea or your favorite plant-based beverage!

Chocolate Espresso Muffins

Yield: 12 muffins

Ingredients:

- 1 1/2 cups (180g) all-purpose flour
- 1/2 cup (50g) cocoa powder
- 1 tablespoon (15g) baking powder
- 1/2 teaspoon (3g) baking soda
- 1/4 teaspoon (1g) salt
- 1 cup (240ml) plant-based milk (such as almond, soy, or oat)
- 1 tablespoon (15ml) apple cider vinegar
- 1/2 cup (120ml) vegetable oil
- 1 cup (200g) granulated sugar
- 2 teaspoons (10g) instant espresso powder or finely ground coffee
- 1 teaspoon (5ml) vanilla extract
- 1 cup (180g) vegan chocolate chips

Gluten-Free Option:

- Substitute all-purpose flour with a gluten-free 1:1 flour blend.
- Add 1/2 teaspoon xanthan gum to the dry ingredients if the 1:1 flour doesn't have xanthan gum included.
- Ensure that the baking powder and baking soda are also gluten-free.

Note:

For an extra boost of chocolate, you can add additional chocolate chips on top of the muffins before baking.

Directions:

1. Preheat the oven to 350°F (175°C). Line a muffin tin with paper liners.
2. In a measuring cup, combine the plant-based milk and apple cider vinegar. Let it sit for about 5 minutes to create a vegan "buttermilk."
3. In a large mixing bowl, whisk together the all-purpose flour, cocoa powder, baking powder, baking soda, and salt.
4. In a separate bowl, mix together the "buttermilk" mixture, vegetable oil, granulated sugar, instant espresso powder or ground coffee, and vanilla extract.
5. Pour the wet ingredients into the dry ingredients and stir until just combined. Do not overmix.
6. Gently fold in the vegan chocolate chips.
7. Spoon the batter into the muffin cups, filling each about 2/3 full.
8. Bake in the preheated oven for 18-22 minutes or until a toothpick inserted into the center of a muffin comes out clean.
9. Allow the muffins to cool in the tin for 5 minutes, then transfer them to a wire rack to cool completely.
10. Serve and savor these indulgent Vegan Chocolate Espresso Muffins with a hot cup of coffee or your favorite plant-based beverage!

Irish Cheddar Spring Onion Biscuits

Yield: Approximately 10-12 biscuits

Ingredients:

- 2 cups (240g) all-purpose flour
- 1 tablespoon (12g) baking powder
- 1/2 teaspoon (3g) baking soda
- 1/2 teaspoon (3g) salt
- 1/2 cup (113g) vegan butter, cold and cubed
- 1 cup (120g) vegan cheddar cheese, shredded
- 1/2 cup (120ml) plant-based buttermilk (1/2 cup plant-based milk + 1 tablespoon apple cider vinegar)
- 1/4 cup (30g) spring onions (green onions), finely chopped
- 1 tablespoon (15ml) Dijon mustard (optional, for extra flavor)

Gluten-Free Option:

- Substitute all-purpose flour with a gluten-free 1:1 flour blend.
- Add 1/2 teaspoon xanthan gum to the dry ingredients if the 1:1 flour doesn't have xanthan gum included.
- Ensure that the baking powder and baking soda are also gluten-free.

Note:

For extra flavor, you can brush the tops of the biscuits with melted vegan butter and sprinkle a little extra shredded Irish cheddar and chopped spring onions before baking.

Directions:

1. Preheat the oven to 425°F (220°C). Line a baking sheet with parchment paper.
2. In a measuring cup, combine the plant-based milk and apple cider vinegar. Let it sit for about 5 minutes to create a vegan "buttermilk."
3. In a large mixing bowl, whisk together the all-purpose flour, baking powder, baking soda, and salt.
4. Add the cold, cubed vegan butter to the flour mixture. Using a pastry cutter or your hands, cut the butter into the flour until the mixture resembles coarse crumbs.
5. Stir in the shredded vegan Irish cheddar cheese and finely chopped spring onions.
6. Add the plant-based buttermilk (and Dijon mustard, if using) to the mixture. Stir until just combined.
7. Turn the dough out onto a floured surface. Gently pat it into a 1-inch thick rectangle.
8. Use a round biscuit cutter to cut out biscuits from the dough. Place the biscuits on the prepared baking sheet, making sure they are close together, almost touching.
9. Bake in the preheated oven for 12-15 minutes or until the biscuits are golden brown.
10. Allow the biscuits to cool on the baking sheet for a few minutes before transferring them to a wire rack.
11. Serve warm and enjoy these delicious Vegan Irish Cheddar Spring Onion Biscuits, perfect for any savory occasion!

CHAPTER 3

Cookies, Brownies, & Bars

Fudge Brownies

Yield: Approximately 16 brownies

Ingredients:

- 1 cup (200g) granulated sugar
- 1/2 cup (120ml) melted coconut oil or vegetable oil
- 2 teaspoons (10ml) vanilla extract
- 1 cup (125g) all-purpose flour
- 1/2 cup (50g) cocoa powder
- 1/2 teaspoon (3g) baking powder
- 1/4 teaspoon (1g) salt
- 1/2 cup (120ml) plant-based milk (such as almond, soy, or oat)
- 1 cup (175g) vegan chocolate chips

Directions:

1. Preheat the oven to 350°F (175°C). Grease or line an 8x8-inch (20x20cm) baking pan.
2. In a large mixing bowl, whisk together the granulated sugar, melted coconut oil (or vegetable oil), and vanilla extract until well combined.
3. In a separate bowl, sift together the all-purpose flour, cocoa powder, baking powder, and salt.
4. Gradually add the dry ingredients to the wet ingredients, stirring until just combined.
5. Add the plant-based milk and continue to stir until the batter is smooth.
6. Fold in the vegan chocolate chips.
7. Pour the batter into the prepared baking pan and spread it evenly.
8. Bake in the preheated oven for 20-25 minutes or until a toothpick inserted into the center comes out with a few moist crumbs (not wet batter).
9. Allow the brownies to cool in the pan for at least 15 minutes before transferring them to a wire rack to cool completely.
10. Once cooled, cut into squares and enjoy these rich and fudgy Vegan Fudge Brownies!
11. Optional: Dust with powdered sugar or serve with a scoop of vegan ice cream.

Gluten-Free Option:

- Substitute all-purpose flour with a gluten-free 1:1 flour blend.
- Add 1/2 teaspoon xanthan gum to the dry ingredients if the 1:1 flour doesn't have xanthan gum included.
- Ensure that the baking powder is also gluten-free.

Peanut Butter Cookie Bars

Yield: Approximately 16 cookie bars

Ingredients:

- For the Cookie Base:
- 1 cup (200g) granulated sugar
- 1/2 cup (120g) vegan butter, softened
- 1/2 cup (125g) smooth peanut butter
- 1 teaspoon (5ml) vanilla extract
- 1 1/2 cups (190g) all-purpose flour
- 1/2 teaspoon (2.5g) baking powder
- 1/4 teaspoon (1g) salt
- 1/4 cup (60ml) plant-based milk (such as almond, soy, or oat)
- For the Peanut Butter Swirl:
- 1/4 cup (60g) smooth peanut butter
- 2 tablespoons (25g) powdered sugar
- 1 tablespoon (15ml) plant-based milk

Directions:

1. Preheat the oven to 350°F (175°C). Grease or line a 9x9-inch (23x23cm) baking pan.
2. In a large mixing bowl, cream together the granulated sugar, softened vegan butter, peanut butter, and vanilla extract until smooth and creamy.
3. In a separate bowl, whisk together the all-purpose flour, baking powder, and salt.
4. Gradually add the dry ingredients to the wet ingredients, mixing until just combined.
5. Add the plant-based milk and mix until a soft cookie dough forms.
6. Press about two-thirds of the cookie dough evenly into the bottom of the prepared baking pan.
7. In a small bowl, mix together the peanut butter, powdered sugar, and plant-based milk for the swirl.
8. Drop spoonfuls of the peanut butter swirl mixture over the cookie dough in the pan.
9. Crumble the remaining cookie dough over the top and gently press it down.
10. Bake in the preheated oven for 20-25 minutes or until the edges are golden brown.
11. Allow the cookie bars to cool in the pan for at least 30 minutes before cutting into squares.
12. Once cooled, cut into squares and enjoy your Vegan Peanut Butter Cookie Bars!

Gluten-Free Option:

- Substitute all-purpose flour with a gluten-free 1:1 flour blend.
- Add 1/2 teaspoon xanthan gum to the dry ingredients if the 1:1 flour doesn't have xanthan gum included.
- Ensure that the baking powder is also gluten-free.

Lemon Bars

Yield: Approximately 16 lemon bars

Ingredients:

- For the Shortbread Crust:
- 1 cup (200g) all-purpose flour
- 1/2 cup (113g) vegan butter, cold and cubed
- 1/4 cup (50g) granulated sugar
- A pinch of salt
- For the Lemon Filling:
- 1 1/4 cups (250g) granulated sugar
- 1/4 cup (30g) all-purpose flour
- 1/2 cup (120ml) fresh lemon juice (from about 3-4 lemons)
- Zest of 2 lemons
- 1/2 cup (120ml) plant-based milk (such as almond, soy, or oat)
- 1/4 cup (30g) powdered sugar, for dusting

Gluten-Free Option:

- Substitute all-purpose flour with a gluten-free 1:1 flour blend.
- Add 1/2 teaspoon xanthan gum to the 1:1 flour if it doesn't have xanthan gum included.

Directions:

1. Preheat the oven to 350°F (175°C). Grease or line an 8x8-inch (20x20cm) baking pan.
2. For the Shortbread Crust:
3. In a food processor or by hand, combine the all-purpose flour, cold cubed vegan butter, granulated sugar, and a pinch of salt. Pulse or mix until the mixture resembles coarse crumbs.
4. Press the mixture into the bottom of the prepared baking pan to form an even crust.
5. Bake the crust in the preheated oven for 15-18 minutes or until it just starts to turn golden around the edges.
6. For the Lemon Filling:
7. In a medium bowl, whisk together the granulated sugar and flour.
8. Add the fresh lemon juice, lemon zest, and plant-based milk. Whisk until well combined.
9. Pour the lemon filling over the baked crust.
10. Bake for an additional 20-25 minutes or until the edges are set, and the center is slightly firm.
11. Allow the lemon bars to cool in the pan for at least 30 minutes.
12. Once cooled, refrigerate for an additional 2 hours to set.
13. Dust the top with powdered sugar before cutting into squares.
14. Cut into squares, and your Vegan Lemon Bars are ready to be enjoyed!

Pumpkin Oatmeal Cookies

Yield: Approximately 24 cookies

Ingredients:

- 1 cup (120g) rolled oats
- 1 cup (120g) all-purpose flour
- 1/2 teaspoon (3g) baking soda
- 1/2 teaspoon (3g) ground cinnamon
- 1/4 teaspoon (1g) ground nutmeg
- 1/4 teaspoon (1g) ground ginger
- 1/4 teaspoon (1g) salt
- 1/2 cup (113g) vegan butter, softened
- 1/2 cup (100g) granulated sugar
- 1/2 cup (100g) packed brown sugar
- 1/2 cup (120g) canned pumpkin puree
- 1 teaspoon (5ml) vanilla extract
- 1/2 cup (80g) raisins or vegan chocolate chips (optional)

Directions:

1. Preheat the oven to 350°F (175°C). Line a baking sheet with parchment paper.
2. In a medium-sized bowl, whisk together the rolled oats, all-purpose flour, baking soda, ground cinnamon, ground nutmeg, ground ginger, and salt. Set aside.
3. In a large mixing bowl, cream together the softened vegan butter, granulated sugar, and brown sugar until light and fluffy.
4. Add the canned pumpkin puree and vanilla extract to the wet ingredients. Mix until well combined.
5. Gradually add the dry ingredients to the wet ingredients, stirring until just combined. If desired, fold in raisins or vegan chocolate chips.
6. Drop rounded tablespoons of dough onto the prepared baking sheet, spacing them about 2 inches apart.
7. Bake in the preheated oven for 12-15 minutes or until the edges are golden brown.
8. Allow the cookies to cool on the baking sheet for a few minutes before transferring them to a wire rack to cool completely.
9. Once cooled, store in an airtight container.
10. Enjoy these delightful Vegan Pumpkin Oatmeal Cookies with a cup of your favorite plant-based milk!

Gluten-Free Option:

- Substitute all-purpose flour with a gluten-free 1:1 flour blend.
- Substitute rolled oats for gluten-free rolled oats
- Add 1/4 teaspoon xanthan gum to the dry ingredients if the 1:1 flour doesn't have xanthan gum included.
- Ensure that the baking soda is also gluten-free.

Carrot Cake Breakfast Cookies

Yield: Approximately 18 cookies

Ingredients:

- 1 cup (120g) rolled oats
- 1 cup (120g) whole wheat flour
- 1 teaspoon (5g) baking powder
- 1/2 teaspoon (3g) ground cinnamon
- 1/4 teaspoon (1g) ground nutmeg
- 1/4 teaspoon (1g) salt
- 1/2 cup (120ml) maple syrup or agave nectar
- 1/4 cup (60ml) coconut oil, melted
- 1 teaspoon (5ml) vanilla extract
- 1 cup (110g) grated carrots
- 1/2 cup (60g) raisins and or chopped walnuts (optional)

Directions:

1. Preheat the oven to 350°F (175°C). Line a baking sheet with parchment paper.
2. In a large bowl, combine the rolled oats, whole wheat flour, baking powder, ground cinnamon, ground nutmeg, and salt.
3. In a separate bowl, whisk together the maple syrup or agave nectar, melted coconut oil, and vanilla extract.
4. Add the wet ingredients to the dry ingredients and mix until well combined.
5. Fold in the grated carrots and, if desired, add raisins or chopped walnuts.
6. Drop rounded tablespoons of dough onto the prepared baking sheet, spacing them about 2 inches apart.
7. Flatten each cookie slightly with the back of a spoon or your fingers.
8. Bake in the preheated oven for 12-15 minutes or until the edges are golden brown.
9. Allow the cookies to cool on the baking sheet for a few minutes before transferring them to a wire rack to cool completely.
10. Store in an airtight container.
11. Enjoy these Vegan Carrot Cake Breakfast Cookies for a tasty and nutritious start to your day!

Gluten-Free Option:

- Substitute whole wheat flour with a gluten-free 1:1 flour blend.
- Add 1/4 teaspoon xanthan gum to the dry ingredients if the 1:1 flour doesn't have xanthan gum included.
- Substitute rolled oats for gluten-free rolled oats
- Ensure that the baking powder is also gluten-free.

Classic Chocolate Chip Cookies

Yield: Approximately 24 cookies

Ingredients:

- 1/2 cup (113g) vegan butter, softened
- 1/2 cup (100g) granulated sugar
- 1/2 cup (100g) packed brown sugar
- 1 teaspoon (5ml) vanilla extract
- 1/4 cup (60ml) plant-based milk (such as almond, soy, or oat)
- 2 cups (240g) all-purpose flour
- 1/2 teaspoon (3g) baking soda
- 1/4 teaspoon (1g) salt
- 1 cup (175g) vegan chocolate chips

Directions:

1. Preheat the oven to 350°F (175°C). Line a baking sheet with parchment paper.
2. In a large mixing bowl, cream together the softened vegan butter, granulated sugar, and brown sugar until light and fluffy.
3. Add the vanilla extract and plant-based milk to the creamed mixture. Mix until well combined.
4. In a separate bowl, whisk together the all-purpose flour, baking soda, and salt.
5. Gradually add the dry ingredients to the wet ingredients, stirring until just combined.
6. Fold in the vegan chocolate chips.
7. Drop rounded tablespoons of cookie dough onto the prepared baking sheet, spacing them about 2 inches apart.
8. Bake in the preheated oven for 10-12 minutes or until the edges are golden brown.
9. Allow the cookies to cool on the baking sheet for a few minutes before transferring them to a wire rack to cool completely.
10. Store in an airtight container.
11. Enjoy these classic Vegan Chocolate Chip Cookies with your favorite plant-based milk or as a sweet treat anytime!

Gluten-Free Option:

- Substitute all-purpose flour with a gluten-free 1:1 flour blend.
- Add 1/2 teaspoon xanthan gum to the dry ingredients if the 1:1 flour doesn't have xanthan gum included.
- Ensure that the baking soda is also gluten-free.

Maple Pecan Bars

Yield: Approximately 16 bars

Ingredients:

- For the Crust:
- 1 cup (120g) all-purpose flour
- 1/2 cup (113g) vegan butter, cold and cubed
- 1/4 cup (50g) granulated sugar
- A pinch of salt
- For the Maple Pecan Filling:
- 1/2 cup (120ml) maple syrup
- 1/3 cup (67g) packed brown sugar
- 1/4 cup (30g) all-purpose flour
- 2 tablespoons (28g) vegan butter, melted
- 1 teaspoon (5ml) vanilla extract
- 1 1/2 cups (180g) chopped pecans

Directions:

1. Preheat the oven to 350°F (175°C). Grease or line a 9x9-inch (23x23cm) baking pan.
2. For the Crust: In a food processor or by hand, combine the all-purpose flour, cold cubed vegan butter, granulated sugar, and a pinch of salt. Pulse or mix until the mixture resembles coarse crumbs.
3. Press the mixture into the bottom of the prepared baking pan to form an even crust.
4. Bake the crust in the preheated oven for 15-18 minutes or until it just starts to turn golden around the edges.
5. For the Maple Pecan Filling: In a medium bowl, whisk together the maple syrup, packed brown sugar, all-purpose flour, melted vegan butter, and vanilla extract.
6. Stir in the chopped pecans until they are evenly coated in the mixture.
7. Pour the maple pecan filling over the baked crust.
8. Bake for an additional 20-25 minutes or until the filling is set.
9. Allow the bars to cool in the pan for at least 30 minutes.
10. Once cooled, refrigerate for an additional 2 hours to set.
11. Cut into squares, and your Vegan Maple Pecan Bars are ready to be enjoyed!
12. Store in an airtight container in the refrigerator.

Gluten-Free Option:

- Substitute all-purpose flour with a gluten-free 1:1 flour blend.
- Add 1/2 teaspoon xanthan gum to the dry ingredients if the 1:1 flour doesn't have xanthan gum included.

Cheesecake Brownies

Yield: Approximately 16 brownies

Ingredients:

- For the Brownie Layer:
- 1 cup (200g) granulated sugar
- 1/2 cup (120ml) vegetable oil
- 1 teaspoon (5ml) vanilla extract
- 1 cup (125g) all-purpose flour
- 1/3 cup (40g) cocoa powder
- 1/2 teaspoon (3g) baking powder
- 1/4 teaspoon (1g) salt
- 1/2 cup (120ml) plant-based milk (such as almond, soy, or oat)
- 1/2 cup (90g) vegan chocolate chips (optional)
- For the Cheesecake Layer:
- 1 cup (225g) vegan cream cheese, softened
- 1/4 cup (50g) granulated sugar
- 1 teaspoon (5ml) vanilla extract
- 1 tablespoon (8g) all-purpose flour

Directions:

1. Preheat the oven to 350°F (175°C). Grease or line an 8x8-inch (20x20cm) baking pan.
2. For the Brownie Layer:
3. In a large mixing bowl, whisk together the granulated sugar, vegetable oil, and vanilla extract.
4. In a separate bowl, sift together the all-purpose flour, cocoa powder, baking powder, and salt.
5. Gradually add the dry ingredients to the wet ingredients, alternating with the plant-based milk, and mix until just combined.
6. Fold in the vegan chocolate chips if using.
7. For the Cheesecake Layer:
8. In another bowl, beat together the softened vegan cream cheese, granulated sugar, vanilla extract, and all-purpose flour until smooth.
9. Assembling:
10. Spread about two-thirds of the brownie batter evenly into the bottom of the prepared baking pan.
11. Spoon dollops of the cheesecake mixture over the brownie layer.
12. Use the remaining brownie batter to cover the cheesecake dollops.
13. Use a knife or skewer to create swirls by gently dragging it through the layers.
14. Bake in the preheated oven for 25-30 minutes or until a toothpick inserted into the center comes out with a few moist crumbs.
15. Allow the cheesecake brownies to cool in the pan for at least 30 minutes before transferring them to a wire rack to cool completely.
16. Once cooled, refrigerate for an additional 2 hours to set.
17. Cut into squares and enjoy these luscious Vegan Cheesecake Brownies!
18. Store in an airtight container in the refrigerator.

Gluten-Free Option:

- Substitute all-purpose flour with a gluten-free 1:1 flour blend.
- Add 1/4 teaspoon xanthan gum to the dry ingredients if the 1:1 flour doesn't have xanthan gum included.
- Ensure that the baking powder is also gluten-free.

Chocolate Cherry Brownies

Yield: Approximately 16 brownies

Ingredients:

- For the Brownie Batter:
- 1 cup (200g) granulated sugar
- 1/2 cup (120ml) vegetable oil
- 1 teaspoon (5ml) vanilla extract
- 1 cup (125g) all-purpose flour
- 1/3 cup (40g) cocoa powder
- 1/2 teaspoon (3g) baking powder
- 1/4 teaspoon (1g) salt
- 1/2 cup (120ml) plant-based milk (such as almond, soy, or oat)
- 1/2 cup (90g) vegan chocolate chips
- For the Cherry Swirl:
- 1 cup (150g) fresh or frozen cherries, pitted and chopped
- 2 tablespoons (30g) granulated sugar
- 1 tablespoon (15ml) water
- 1 tablespoon (8g) cornstarch

Directions:

1. Preheat the oven to 350°F (175°C). Grease or line an 8x8-inch (20x20cm) baking pan.
2. For the Brownie Batter: In a large mixing bowl, whisk together the granulated sugar, vegetable oil, and vanilla extract.
3. In a separate bowl, sift together the all-purpose flour, cocoa powder, baking powder, and salt.
4. Gradually add the dry ingredients to the wet ingredients, alternating with the plant-based milk, and mix until just combined.
5. Fold in the vegan chocolate chips.
6. For the Cherry Swirl: In a saucepan, combine the chopped cherries, granulated sugar, water, and cornstarch.
7. Cook over medium heat, stirring continuously, until the mixture thickens and the cherries break down, creating a syrupy consistency. This usually takes about 5-7 minutes.
8. Remove the cherry swirl from heat and let it cool slightly.
9. Assembling: Spread about two-thirds of the brownie batter evenly into the bottom of the prepared baking pan.
10. Spoon dollops of the cherry swirl mixture over the brownie layer.
11. Use the remaining brownie batter to cover the cherry swirl dollops.
12. Use a knife or skewer to create swirls by gently dragging it through the layers.
13. Bake in the preheated oven for 25-30 minutes or until a toothpick inserted into the center comes out with a few moist crumbs.
14. Allow the chocolate cherry brownies to cool in the pan for at least 30 minutes before transferring them to a wire rack to cool completely.
15. Once cooled, cut into squares and indulge in these delightful Vegan Chocolate Cherry Brownies!
16. Store in an airtight container.

Gluten-Free Option:

- Substitute all-purpose flour with a gluten-free 1:1 flour blend.
- Add 1/4 teaspoon xanthan gum to the dry ingredients if the 1:1 flour doesn't have xanthan gum included.
- Ensure that the baking powder is also gluten-free.

Dark Chocolate Chambord Brownies

Yield: Approximately 16 brownies

Ingredients:

- For the Brownie Batter:
- 1 cup (200g) granulated sugar
- 1/2 cup (120ml) vegetable oil
- 1 teaspoon (5ml) vanilla extract
- 1 cup (125g) all-purpose flour
- 1/3 cup (40g) dark cocoa powder
- 1/2 teaspoon (3g) baking powder
- 1/4 teaspoon (1g) salt
- 1/2 cup (120ml) plant-based milk (such as almond, soy, or oat)
- 1/2 cup (90g) vegan dark chocolate chips
- For the Chambord Ganache:
- 1/2 cup (120ml) plant-based heavy cream (coconut cream works well)
- 1 cup (175g) vegan dark chocolate, finely chopped
- 2 tablespoons (30ml) Chambord liqueur (or any other berry-flavored liqueur)

Directions:

1. Preheat the oven to 350°F (175°C). Grease or line an 8x8-inch (20x20cm) baking pan.
2. For the Brownie Batter: In a large mixing bowl, whisk together the granulated sugar, vegetable oil, and vanilla extract.
3. In a separate bowl, sift together the all-purpose flour, dark cocoa powder, baking powder, and salt.
4. Gradually add the dry ingredients to the wet ingredients, alternating with the plant-based milk, and mix until just combined.
5. Fold in the vegan dark chocolate chips.
6. For the Chambord Ganache: In a small saucepan, heat the plant-based heavy cream until it just begins to simmer. Remove from heat.
7. Add the finely chopped vegan dark chocolate to the heated cream and let it sit for a minute.
8. Stir the chocolate and cream together until smooth and well combined.
9. Mix in the Chambord liqueur until fully incorporated.
10. Assembling: Spread the brownie batter evenly into the bottom of the prepared baking pan.
11. Pour the Chambord ganache over the brownie batter.
12. Use a knife or skewer to create swirls by gently dragging it through the layers.
13. Bake in the preheated oven for 25-30 minutes or until a toothpick inserted into the center comes out with a few moist crumbs.
14. Allow the dark chocolate Chambord brownies to cool in the pan for at least 30 minutes before transferring them to a wire rack to cool completely.
15. Once cooled, cut into squares and savor these rich and sophisticated Vegan Dark Chocolate Chambord Brownies!
16. Store in an airtight container. Enjoy responsibly!

Gluten-Free Option:

- Substitute all-purpose flour with a gluten-free 1:1 flour blend.
- Add 1/4 teaspoon xanthan gum to the dry ingredients if the 1:1 flour doesn't have xanthan gum included.
- Ensure that the baking powder is also gluten-free.

No-Bake Cookie Dough Bars

Yield: Approximately 16 bars

Ingredients:

- For the Cookie Dough Base:
- 1 1/2 cups (180g) almond flour
- 1/2 cup (120ml) maple syrup
- 1/4 cup (60g) coconut oil, melted
- 1 teaspoon (5ml) vanilla extract
- 1/4 teaspoon (1g) salt
- 1/2 cup (90g) vegan chocolate chips
- For the Chocolate Topping:
- 1 cup (175g) vegan chocolate chips
- 2 tablespoons (30g) coconut oil

Directions:

1. For the Cookie Dough Base:
2. In a large mixing bowl, combine the almond flour, maple syrup, melted coconut oil, vanilla extract, and salt.
3. Mix until well combined and a dough forms.
4. Fold in the vegan chocolate chips.
5. Press the cookie dough mixture into the bottom of an 8x8-inch (20x20cm) square pan lined with parchment paper, creating an even layer.
6. For the Chocolate Topping:
7. In a microwave-safe bowl, melt the vegan chocolate chips and coconut oil together in 20-second intervals, stirring in between, until smooth.
8. Pour the melted chocolate over the cookie dough layer, spreading it evenly with a spatula.
9. Place the pan in the refrigerator for at least 2 hours to allow the bars to set.
10. Once set, lift the bars out of the pan using the parchment paper and place them on a cutting board.
11. Using a sharp knife, cut the bars into squares.
12. Serve and enjoy these delicious Vegan No-Bake Cookie Dough Bars straight from the fridge!
13. Store any remaining bars in an airtight container in the refrigerator.

Chocolate Hazelnut Thumbprint Cookies

Yield: Approximately 20 cookies

Ingredients:

- For the Cookie Dough:
- 1 cup (120g) all-purpose flour
- 1/2 cup (50g) almond flour
- 1/2 cup (120g) vegan butter, softened
- 1/4 cup (50g) granulated sugar
- 1 teaspoon (5ml) vanilla extract
- 1/4 teaspoon (1.25g) salt
- For the Chocolate Hazelnut Filling:
- 1/2 cup (150g) vegan chocolate hazelnut spread
- For the Topping:
- 1/4 cup (30g) chopped hazelnuts

Directions:

1. Preheat the oven to 350°F (175°C). Line a baking sheet with parchment paper.
2. For the Cookie Dough: In a large mixing bowl, cream together the vegan butter, granulated sugar, and vanilla extract until smooth.
3. In a separate bowl, whisk together the all-purpose flour, almond flour, and salt.
4. Gradually add the dry ingredients to the wet ingredients, mixing until just combined.
5. Form the dough into small balls, about 1 inch in diameter, and place them on the prepared baking sheet.
6. Use your thumb or the back of a teaspoon to create an indentation in the center of each cookie.
7. Bake in the preheated oven for 10-12 minutes or until the edges are golden.
8. Allow the cookies to cool on the baking sheet for a few minutes before transferring them to a wire rack to cool completely.
9. For the Chocolate Hazelnut Filling:
10. Once the cookies are cooled, spoon a small amount of vegan chocolate hazelnut spread into the indentation of each cookie.
11. For the Topping: Sprinkle chopped hazelnuts on top of the chocolate hazelnut spread, gently pressing them into the filling.
12. Allow the filling to set before serving or storing.
13. Enjoy these delectable Vegan Chocolate Hazelnut Thumbprint Cookies with a cup of your favorite plant-based milk!

Gluten-Free Option:

- Substitute all-purpose flour with a gluten-free 1:1 flour blend.
- Add 1/4 teaspoon xanthan gum to the dry ingredients if the 1:1 flour doesn't have xanthan gum included.

Sugar Cookies

Yield: Approximately 24 cookies

Ingredients:

- For the Sugar Cookie Dough:
- 2 1/2 cups (315g) all-purpose flour
- 1 cup (225g) vegan butter, softened
- 1 cup (200g) granulated sugar
- 1 teaspoon (5ml) vanilla extract
- 1/2 teaspoon (3g) baking powder
- 1/4 teaspoon (1g) salt
- For Decorating:
- Vegan royal icing (store-bought or homemade)
- Vegan food coloring (optional)
- Sprinkles or decorations of your choice

Directions:

1. Preheat the oven to 350°F (175°C). Line baking sheets with parchment paper.
2. For the Sugar Cookie Dough:
3. In a large mixing bowl, cream together the softened vegan butter, granulated sugar, and vanilla extract until smooth.
4. In a separate bowl, whisk together the all-purpose flour, baking powder, and salt.
5. Gradually add the dry ingredients to the wet ingredients, mixing until just combined. Do not overmix.
6. Divide the dough into two portions, wrap each in plastic wrap, and refrigerate for at least 30 minutes.
7. On a lightly floured surface, roll out one portion of the chilled dough to about 1/4 inch (0.6 cm) thickness.
8. Use cookie cutters to cut out shapes and place them on the prepared baking sheets.
9. Repeat the rolling and cutting process with the second portion of dough.
10. Bake in the preheated oven for 8-10 minutes or until the edges are just beginning to turn golden. Be careful not to overbake.
11. Allow the cookies to cool on the baking sheets for a few minutes before transferring them to a wire rack to cool completely.
12. For Decorating:
13. Once the cookies are completely cooled, prepare vegan royal icing according to package instructions or your chosen recipe.
14. Divide the icing into bowls and add vegan food coloring if desired.
15. Decorate the cookies with the royal icing and add sprinkles or decorations while the icing is still wet.
16. Allow the icing to set before storing or serving.
17. Enjoy these Vegan Sugar Cookies as a delightful treat or as beautifully decorated gifts!

Gluten-Free Option:

- Substitute all-purpose flour with a gluten-free 1:1 flour blend.
- Add 1/2 teaspoon xanthan gum to the dry ingredients if the 1:1 flour doesn't have xanthan gum included.
- Ensure that the baking powder is also gluten-free.

Double Chocolate Sea Salt Cookies

Yield: Approximately 24 cookies

Ingredients:

- For the Cookie Dough:
- 1 cup (125g) all-purpose flour
- 1/3 cup (40g) cocoa powder
- 1/2 teaspoon (2.5g) baking soda
- 1/4 teaspoon (1.25g) salt
- 1/2 cup (120g) vegan butter, softened
- 1/2 cup (100g) granulated sugar
- 1/4 cup (50g) brown sugar, packed
- 1 teaspoon (5ml) vanilla extract
- 1/4 cup (60ml) plant-based milk (such as almond, soy, or oat)
- 1 cup (175g) vegan chocolate chips or chunks
- For Topping:
- Flaky sea salt

Directions:

1. Preheat the oven to 350°F (175°C). Line baking sheets with parchment paper.
2. For the Cookie Dough: In a medium bowl, whisk together the all-purpose flour, cocoa powder, baking soda, and salt.
3. In a large mixing bowl, cream together the softened vegan butter, granulated sugar, brown sugar, and vanilla extract until smooth.
4. Gradually add the dry ingredients to the wet ingredients, alternating with the plant-based milk, and mix until just combined.
5. Fold in the vegan chocolate chips or chunks.
6. Drop rounded tablespoons of dough onto the prepared baking sheets, spacing them about 2 inches apart.
7. Flatten each cookie slightly with the back of a spoon or your fingers.
8. Bake in the preheated oven for 10-12 minutes or until the edges are set.
9. Remove from the oven and immediately sprinkle a pinch of flaky sea salt on top of each cookie.
10. Allow the cookies to cool on the baking sheets for a few minutes before transferring them to a wire rack to cool completely.
11. Once cooled, store in an airtight container.
12. Enjoy these indulgent Vegan Double Chocolate Sea Salt Cookies with a glass of plant-based milk or your favorite beverage!

Gluten-Free Option:

- Substitute all-purpose flour with a gluten-free 1:1 flour blend.
- Add 1/4 teaspoon xanthan gum to the dry ingredients if the 1:1 flour doesn't have xanthan gum included.
- Ensure that the baking soda is also gluten-free.

Gingerbread Oatmeal Creampie Cookies

Yield: Approximately 16 sandwich cookies

Ingredients:

- For the Gingerbread Oatmeal Cookies:
- 1 cup (120g) rolled oats
- 1 cup (125g) all-purpose flour
- 1 teaspoon (5g) ground ginger
- 1/2 teaspoon (2.5g) ground cinnamon
- 1/4 teaspoon (1.25g) ground cloves
- 1/4 teaspoon (1.25g) salt
- 1/2 cup (120g) vegan butter, softened
- 1/2 cup (100g) brown sugar, packed
- 1/4 cup (60ml) molasses
- 1 teaspoon (5ml) vanilla extract
- For the Cream Filling:
- 1/2 cup (120g) vegan cream cheese
- 1/4 cup (60g) powdered sugar
- 1/2 teaspoon (2.5ml) vanilla extract

Directions:

1. Preheat the oven to 350°F (175°C). Line baking sheets with parchment paper.
2. For the Gingerbread Oatmeal Cookies: In a medium bowl, combine rolled oats, all-purpose flour, ground ginger, ground cinnamon, ground cloves, and salt.
3. In a large mixing bowl, cream together the softened vegan butter and brown sugar until light and fluffy.
4. Add molasses and vanilla extract to the wet ingredients, mixing until well combined.
5. Gradually add the dry ingredients to the wet ingredients, mixing until just combined.
6. Drop rounded tablespoons of dough onto the prepared baking sheets, spacing them about 2 inches apart.
7. Flatten each cookie slightly with the back of a spoon or your fingers.
8. Bake in the preheated oven for 10-12 minutes or until the edges are set.
9. Allow the cookies to cool on the baking sheets for a few minutes before transferring them to a wire rack to cool completely.
10. For the Cream Filling: In a medium bowl, beat together vegan cream cheese, powdered sugar, and vanilla extract until smooth.
11. Assembly: Once the cookies are completely cooled, spread a generous amount of cream filling on the bottom of one cookie and top it with another, creating a sandwich.
12. Repeat with the remaining cookies.
13. Store in an airtight container in the refrigerator.
14. Substitute all-purpose flour with a gluten-free 1:1 flour blend.
15. Add 1/4 teaspoon xanthan gum to the dry ingredients if the 1:1 flour doesn't have xanthan gum included.
16. Ensure that the baking soda is also gluten-free.

Gluten-Free Option:

- Substitute all-purpose flour with a gluten-free 1:1 flour blend.
- Substitute rolled oats for gluten-free rolled oats
- Add 1/4 teaspoon xanthan gum to the dry ingredients if the 1:1 flour doesn't have xanthan gum included.

Ginger Molasses Cookies

Yield: Approximately 24 cookies

Ingredients:

- 2 cups (250g) all-purpose flour
- 2 teaspoons (10g) baking soda
- 1/2 teaspoon (3g) salt
- 1 teaspoon (5g) ground ginger
- 1 teaspoon (5g) ground cinnamon
- 1/2 teaspoon (3g) ground cloves
- 3/4 cup (170g) vegan butter, softened
- 1 cup (200g) granulated sugar
- 1/4 cup (60ml) molasses
- 1 flax egg (1 tablespoon ground flaxseed + 3 tablespoons water)
- 1 teaspoon (5ml) vanilla extract
- Granulated sugar for rolling

Directions:

1. Preheat the oven to 350°F (175°C). Line baking sheets with parchment paper.
2. In a medium bowl, whisk together the all-purpose flour, baking soda, salt, ground ginger, ground cinnamon, and ground cloves.
3. In a large mixing bowl, cream together the softened vegan butter and granulated sugar until light and fluffy.
4. Prepare the flax egg by mixing ground flaxseed with water in a small bowl. Let it sit for 5 minutes to thicken.
5. Add the molasses, prepared flax egg, and vanilla extract to the creamed mixture. Mix until well combined.
6. Gradually add the dry ingredients to the wet ingredients, mixing until just combined.
7. Chill the dough in the refrigerator for at least 30 minutes to make it easier to handle.
8. Scoop tablespoon-sized portions of dough and roll them into balls. Roll each ball in granulated sugar to coat.
9. Place the coated dough balls on the prepared baking sheets, spacing them about 2 inches apart.
10. Bake in the preheated oven for 10-12 minutes or until the edges are set.
11. Allow the cookies to cool on the baking sheets for a few minutes before transferring them to a wire rack to cool completely.
12. Once cooled, store in an airtight container.
13. Enjoy these classic Vegan Ginger Molasses Cookies with a cup of tea or coffee!

Gluten-Free Option:

- Substitute all-purpose flour with a gluten-free 1:1 flour blend.
- Add 1/2 teaspoon xanthan gum to the dry ingredients if the 1:1 flour doesn't have xanthan gum included.
- Ensure that the baking soda is also gluten-free.

Vanilla Wafers

Yield: Approximately 36 cookies

Ingredients:

- 1 1/2 cups (190g) all-purpose flour
- 1/2 cup (60g) cornstarch
- 1/2 teaspoon (3g) baking powder
- 1/4 teaspoon (1g) salt
- 1 cup (225g) vegan butter, softened
- 1 cup (200g) granulated sugar
- 1 teaspoon (5ml) vanilla extract

Directions:

1. Preheat the oven to 350°F (175°C). Line baking sheets with parchment paper.
2. In a medium bowl, whisk together the all-purpose flour, cornstarch, baking powder, and salt.
3. In a large mixing bowl, cream together the softened vegan butter and granulated sugar until light and fluffy.
4. Add the vanilla extract to the creamed mixture and mix until well combined.
5. Gradually add the dry ingredients to the wet ingredients, mixing until just combined.
6. Scoop tablespoon-sized portions of dough and roll them into balls. Place the dough balls on the prepared baking sheets, spacing them about 2 inches apart.
7. Use the back of a fork to gently flatten each dough ball.
8. Bake in the preheated oven for 10-12 minutes or until the edges are set and the bottoms are lightly golden.
9. Allow the cookies to cool on the baking sheets for a few minutes before transferring them to a wire rack to cool completely.
10. Once cooled, store in an airtight container.
11. Enjoy these classic Vegan Vanilla Wafers on their own or use them in your favorite recipes that call for vanilla wafers!

Gluten-Free Option:

- Substitute all-purpose flour with a gluten-free 1:1 flour blend.
- Add 1/2 teaspoon xanthan gum to the dry ingredients if the 1:1 flour doesn't have xanthan gum included.
- Ensure that the baking powder is also gluten-free.

Almond Anise Biscotti

Yield: Approximately 24 biscotti

Ingredients:

- 2 cups (250g) all-purpose flour
- 1 cup (200g) granulated sugar
- 1 teaspoon (5g) baking powder
- 1/4 teaspoon (1g) salt
- 1/2 cup (120ml) vegetable oil
- 1/4 cup (60ml) almond milk
- 1 teaspoon (5ml) vanilla extract
- 1 teaspoon (5ml) almond extract
- 1 teaspoon (5ml) anise extract
- 1 cup (125g) whole almonds, toasted
- Zest of 1 lemon

Directions:

1. Preheat the oven to 350°F (175°C). Line a baking sheet with parchment paper.
2. In a large bowl, whisk together the all-purpose flour, granulated sugar, baking powder, and salt.
3. In a separate bowl, combine the vegetable oil, almond milk, vanilla extract, almond extract, and anise extract.
4. Add the wet ingredients to the dry ingredients, mixing until a dough forms.
5. Fold in the toasted whole almonds and lemon zest until evenly distributed throughout the dough.
6. Divide the dough in half. On a lightly floured surface, shape each half into a log, approximately 12 inches long and 2 inches wide.
7. Place the logs on the prepared baking sheet, leaving space between them.
8. Bake in the preheated oven for 25-30 minutes or until the logs are lightly golden and firm to the touch.
9. Allow the logs to cool for about 15 minutes, then use a serrated knife to cut them into slices, about 1/2 inch thick.
10. Place the sliced biscotti back on the baking sheet, cut side down, and bake for an additional 15-20 minutes or until they are golden and crisp.
11. Allow the biscotti to cool completely on a wire rack.
12. Store in an airtight container.
13. Enjoy these Vegan Almond Anise Biscotti with your favorite hot beverage or as a delightful after-dinner treat!

Gluten-Free Option:

- Substitute all-purpose flour with a gluten-free 1:1 flour blend.
- Add 1/2 teaspoon xanthan gum to the dry ingredients if the 1:1 flour doesn't have xanthan gum included.
- Ensure that the baking powder is also gluten-free.

Red Velvet Sandwich Cookies

Yield: Approximately 24 sandwich cookies

Ingredients:

- For the Red Velvet Cookies:
- 2 cups (250g) all-purpose flour
- 1/4 cup (30g) cocoa powder
- 1 teaspoon (5g) baking soda
- 1/4 teaspoon (1g) salt
- 1 cup (200g) granulated sugar
- 1/2 cup (120ml) vegetable oil
- 1/4 cup (60ml) unsweetened applesauce
- 1 tablespoon (15ml) red food coloring
- 1 teaspoon (5ml) vanilla extract
- 1 teaspoon (5ml) white or apple cider vinegar
- For the Cream Cheese Filling:
- 1/2 cup (112g) vegan cream cheese, softened
- 1/4 cup (60g) vegan butter, softened
- 2 cups (250g) powdered sugar
- 1 teaspoon (5ml) vanilla extract

Directions:

1. Preheat the oven to 350°F (175°C). Line baking sheets with parchment paper.
2. For the Red Velvet Cookies:
3. In a medium bowl, whisk together the all-purpose flour, cocoa powder, baking soda, and salt.
4. In a large mixing bowl, whisk together the granulated sugar, vegetable oil, applesauce, red food coloring, vanilla extract, and white or apple cider vinegar until well combined.
5. Gradually add the dry ingredients to the wet ingredients, mixing until just combined.
6. Drop rounded tablespoons of dough onto the prepared baking sheets, spacing them about 2 inches apart.
7. Flatten each cookie slightly with the back of a spoon or your fingers.
8. Bake in the preheated oven for 10-12 minutes or until the edges are set.
9. Allow the cookies to cool on the baking sheets for a few minutes before transferring them to a wire rack to cool completely.
10. For the Cream Cheese Filling:
11. In a medium bowl, beat together the softened vegan cream cheese, softened vegan butter, powdered sugar, and vanilla extract until smooth.
12. Assembly:
13. Once the cookies are completely cooled, spread a generous amount of cream cheese filling on the bottom of one cookie and top it with another, creating a sandwich.
14. Repeat with the remaining cookies.
15. Store in an airtight container in the refrigerator.
16. Enjoy these Vegan Red Velvet Sandwich Cookies with a glass of plant-based milk or your favorite beverage!

Gluten-Free Option:

- Substitute all-purpose flour with a gluten-free 1:1 flour blend.
- Add 1/2 teaspoon xanthan gum to the dry ingredients if the 1:1 flour doesn't have xanthan gum included.
- Ensure that the baking soda is also gluten-free.

Shortbread Cookies

Yield: Approximately 24 cookies

Ingredients:

- 1 cup (225g) vegan butter, softened
- 1/2 cup (100g) granulated sugar
- 2 cups (250g) all-purpose flour
- 1/4 teaspoon (1.25g) salt
- 1 teaspoon (5ml) vanilla extract (optional)

Directions:

1. Preheat the oven to 350°F (175°C). Line baking sheets with parchment paper.
2. In a large mixing bowl, cream together the softened vegan butter and granulated sugar until light and fluffy.
3. Add the vanilla extract (if using) and mix until well combined.
4. In a separate bowl, whisk together the all-purpose flour and salt.
5. Gradually add the dry ingredients to the wet ingredients, mixing until just combined. Do not overmix.
6. Form the dough into a disk, wrap it in plastic wrap, and refrigerate for at least 30 minutes.
7. On a lightly floured surface, roll out the chilled dough to about 1/4 inch (0.6 cm) thickness.
8. Use cookie cutters to cut out shapes and place them on the prepared baking sheets, leaving space between each cookie.
9. Optional: Use a fork to create a decorative pattern on the cookies by gently pressing down.
10. Bake in the preheated oven for 12-15 minutes or until the edges are lightly golden.
11. Allow the cookies to cool on the baking sheets for a few minutes before transferring them to a wire rack to cool completely.
12. Once cooled, store in an airtight container.
13. Enjoy these classic Vegan Shortbread Cookies with a cup of tea or coffee!

Lemon Crinkle Cookies

Yield: Approximately 24 cookies

Ingredients:

- 2 cups (250g) all-purpose flour
- 1 teaspoon (5g) baking powder
- 1/2 teaspoon (3g) baking soda
- 1/4 teaspoon (1g) salt
- 1 cup (200g) granulated sugar
- 1/3 cup (80ml) vegetable oil
- Zest of 2 lemons
- 1/4 cup (60ml) fresh lemon juice
- 1 teaspoon (5ml) vanilla extract
- 1/2 cup (60g) powdered sugar, for rolling

Directions:

1. Preheat the oven to 350°F (175°C). Line baking sheets with parchment paper.
2. In a medium bowl, whisk together the all-purpose flour, baking powder, baking soda, and salt.
3. In a large mixing bowl, whisk together the granulated sugar, vegetable oil, lemon zest, lemon juice, and vanilla extract until well combined.
4. Gradually add the dry ingredients to the wet ingredients, mixing until just combined.
5. Chill the dough in the refrigerator for at least 30 minutes to make it easier to handle.
6. Place the powdered sugar in a shallow bowl.
7. Scoop tablespoon-sized portions of dough and roll them into balls. Roll each ball in powdered sugar to coat.
8. Place the coated dough balls on the prepared baking sheets, spacing them about 2 inches apart.
9. Bake in the preheated oven for 10-12 minutes or until the edges are set and the tops have cracked.
10. Allow the cookies to cool on the baking sheets for a few minutes before transferring them to a wire rack to cool completely.
11. Once cooled, store in an airtight container.

Gluten-Free Option:

- Substitute all-purpose flour with a gluten-free 1:1 flour blend.
- Add 1/2 teaspoon xanthan gum to the dry ingredients if the 1:1 flour doesn't have xanthan gum included.
- Ensure that the baking soda and baking powder is also gluten-free.

Pecan Snowball Cookies

Yield: Approximately 24 cookies

Ingredients:

- 1 cup (225g) vegan butter, softened
- 1/2 cup (60g) powdered sugar
- 2 teaspoons (10ml) vanilla extract
- 2 cups (250g) all-purpose flour
- 1/4 teaspoon (1g) salt
- 1 cup (120g) pecans, finely chopped
- Additional powdered sugar, for rolling

Directions:

1. Preheat the oven to 350°F (175°C). Line baking sheets with parchment paper.
2. In a large mixing bowl, cream together the softened vegan butter, powdered sugar, and vanilla extract until light and fluffy.
3. In a separate bowl, whisk together the all-purpose flour and salt.
4. Gradually add the dry ingredients to the wet ingredients, mixing until just combined.
5. Fold in the finely chopped pecans until evenly distributed throughout the dough.
6. Shape the dough into tablespoon-sized balls and place them on the prepared baking sheets, spacing them about 2 inches apart.
7. Bake in the preheated oven for 12-15 minutes or until the bottoms are lightly golden.
8. Allow the cookies to cool on the baking sheets for a few minutes before transferring them to a wire rack to cool completely.
9. Once cooled, roll each cookie in additional powdered sugar to coat generously.
10. Store in an airtight container.
11. Enjoy these classic Vegan Pecan Snowball Cookies, also known as Mexican Wedding Cookies or Russian Tea Cakes!

Gluten-Free Option:

- Substitute all-purpose flour with a gluten-free 1:1 flour blend.
- Add 1/2 teaspoon xanthan gum to the dry ingredients if the 1:1 flour doesn't have xanthan gum included.

Apricot Pistachio Oat Bars

Yield: Approximately 16 bars

Ingredients:

- For the Oat Base:
- 2 cups (200g) rolled oats
- 1 cup (120g) all-purpose flour
- 1/2 cup (100g) brown sugar, packed
- 1/2 teaspoon (2.5g) baking soda
- 1/4 teaspoon (1.25g) salt
- 1 cup (225g) vegan butter, melted
- For the Apricot Pistachio Filling:
- 1 1/2 cups (200g) dried apricots, chopped
- 1 cup (120g) shelled pistachios, chopped
- 1/2 cup (120ml) water
- 1/4 cup (60ml) maple syrup
- Zest and juice of 1 orange

Directions:

1. Preheat the oven to 350°F (175°C). Line a 9x9-inch (23x23cm) baking pan with parchment paper, leaving an overhang on two opposite sides for easy removal.
2. For the Oat Base: In a large bowl, combine the rolled oats, all-purpose flour, brown sugar, baking soda, and salt.
3. Add the melted vegan butter to the dry ingredients and mix until well combined.
4. Press two-thirds of the oat mixture into the bottom of the prepared baking pan to create an even base.
5. For the Apricot Pistachio Filling: In a saucepan, combine the chopped dried apricots, chopped pistachios, water, maple syrup, orange zest, and orange juice.
6. Cook over medium heat, stirring frequently, until the mixture thickens and the apricots soften, about 10-12 minutes.
7. Spread the apricot pistachio filling evenly over the oat base in the baking pan.
8. Crumble the remaining oat mixture over the top of the filling, creating a crumbly topping.
9. Bake in the preheated oven for 25-30 minutes or until the top is golden brown.
10. Allow the bars to cool completely in the pan before using the parchment paper overhang to lift them out.
11. Once cooled, cut into squares or bars.
12. Store in an airtight container.
13. Enjoy these Vegan Apricot Pistachio Oat Bars as a wholesome and delicious snack or dessert!

Gluten-Free Option:

- Substitute all-purpose flour with a gluten-free 1:1 flour blend.
- Substitute rolled oats for gluten-free rolled oats
- Add 1/4 teaspoon xanthan gum to the dry ingredients if the 1:1 flour doesn't have xanthan gum included.
- Ensure that the baking soda is also gluten-free.

CHAPTER 4

Bread

Banana Bread

Yield: 1 loaf

Ingredients:

- 3 ripe bananas, mashed
- 1/2 cup (120ml) vegetable oil or melted coconut oil
- 1/2 cup (100g) brown sugar, packed
- 1/4 cup (60ml) maple syrup
- 1 teaspoon (5ml) vanilla extract
- 2 cups (250g) all-purpose flour
- 1 teaspoon (5g) baking soda
- 1/2 teaspoon (3g) baking powder
- 1/2 teaspoon (3g) salt
- 1/2 cup (60g) vegan chocolate chips (optional)
- 1/2 cup (60g) chopped walnuts (optional)
- 2 tablespoons (20g) pumpkin seeds (pepitas), for topping

Directions:

1. Preheat the oven to 350°F (175°C). Grease a 9x5-inch (23x13cm) loaf pan.
2. In a large mixing bowl, combine the mashed bananas, vegetable oil or melted coconut oil, brown sugar, maple syrup, and vanilla extract. Mix until well combined.
3. In a separate bowl, whisk together the all-purpose flour, baking soda, baking powder, and salt.
4. Gradually add the dry ingredients to the wet ingredients, mixing until just combined. Do not overmix.
5. If using, fold in the vegan chocolate chips and chopped walnuts until evenly distributed in the batter.
6. Pour the batter into the prepared loaf pan, spreading it evenly.
7. Sprinkle pumpkin seeds (pepitas) over the top of the batter.
8. Bake in the preheated oven for 50-60 minutes or until a toothpick inserted into the center comes out clean or with a few moist crumbs.
9. If the top is browning too quickly, you can loosely tent it with aluminum foil during the last 15 minutes of baking.
10. Allow the banana bread to cool in the pan for 10 minutes before transferring it to a wire rack to cool completely.
11. Once cooled, slice and enjoy.

Gluten-Free Option:

- Substitute all-purpose flour with a gluten-free 1:1 flour blend.
- Add 1/2 teaspoon xanthan gum to the dry ingredients if the 1:1 flour doesn't have xanthan gum included.
- Ensure that the baking soda and baking powder are also gluten-free.

Lemon Pistachio Bread

Yield: 1 loaf

Ingredients:

- For the Bread:
- 2 cups (250g) all-purpose flour
- 1 cup (200g) granulated sugar
- 1 teaspoon (5g) baking powder
- 1/2 teaspoon (2.5g) baking soda
- 1/4 teaspoon (1.25g) salt
- 1 cup (240ml) non-dairy milk (such as almond or soy)
- 1/3 cup (80ml) vegetable oil
- 1/4 cup (60ml) fresh lemon juice
- Zest of 2 lemons
- 1 teaspoon (5ml) vanilla extract
- 1 cup (120g) shelled pistachios, finely chopped
- For the Pistachio Glaze:
- 1/2 cup (60g) shelled pistachios, finely chopped
- 1 cup (120g) powdered sugar
- 2-3 tablespoons (30-45ml) fresh lemon juice
- Lemon zest for garnish (optional)

Gluten-Free Option:

- Substitute all-purpose flour with a gluten-free 1:1 flour blend.
- Add 1/2 teaspoon xanthan gum to the dry ingredients if the 1:1 flour doesn't have xanthan gum included.
- Ensure that the baking soda and baking powder are also gluten-free.

Directions:

1. Preheat the oven to 350°F (175°C). Grease a 9x5-inch (23x13cm) loaf pan.
2. For the Bread:
3. In a large mixing bowl, whisk together the all-purpose flour, granulated sugar, baking powder, baking soda, and salt.
4. In a separate bowl, whisk together the non-dairy milk, vegetable oil, fresh lemon juice, lemon zest, and vanilla extract.
5. Gradually add the wet ingredients to the dry ingredients, mixing until just combined. Do not overmix. Fold in the chopped pistachios.
6. Pour the batter into the prepared loaf pan, spreading it evenly.
7. Bake in the preheated oven for 45-55 minutes or until a toothpick inserted into the center comes out clean or with a few moist crumbs.
8. Allow the bread to cool in the pan for 10 minutes before transferring it to a wire rack to cool completely.
9. For the Pistachio Glaze:
10. In a small bowl, mix together the finely chopped pistachios, powdered sugar, and fresh lemon juice until you have a thick glaze.
11. Once the bread has cooled, drizzle the pistachio glaze over the top.
12. Optionally, garnish with additional lemon zest for a burst of citrus flavor.
13. Allow the glaze to set before slicing and serving.
14. Enjoy this Vegan Lemon Pistachio Bread as a delightful tea-time treat or a flavorful dessert!

Pumpkin Chocolate Chip Bread

Yield: 1 loaf

Ingredients:

- 1 3/4 cups (220g) all-purpose flour
- 1 teaspoon (5g) baking soda
- 1/2 teaspoon (3g) baking powder
- 1/2 teaspoon (3g) salt
- 1 teaspoon (2g) ground cinnamon
- 1/2 teaspoon (1g) ground nutmeg
- 1/4 teaspoon (1g) ground cloves
- 1/4 teaspoon (1g) ground ginger
- 1 cup (240ml) canned pumpkin puree
- 1/2 cup (120ml) vegetable oil or melted coconut oil
- 1 cup (200g) granulated sugar
- 1/2 cup (120ml) non-dairy milk (such as almond or soy)
- 1 teaspoon (5ml) vanilla extract
- 1 cup (175g) vegan chocolate chips

Directions:

1. Preheat the oven to 350°F (175°C). Grease a 9x5-inch (23x13cm) loaf pan.
2. In a large mixing bowl, whisk together the all-purpose flour, baking soda, baking powder, salt, ground cinnamon, ground nutmeg, ground cloves, and ground ginger.
3. In another bowl, mix together the canned pumpkin puree, vegetable oil or melted coconut oil, granulated sugar, non-dairy milk, and vanilla extract until well combined.
4. Gradually add the wet ingredients to the dry ingredients, mixing until just combined. Do not overmix.
5. Fold in the vegan chocolate chips until evenly distributed in the batter.
6. Pour the batter into the prepared loaf pan, spreading it evenly.
7. Bake in the preheated oven for 55-65 minutes or until a toothpick inserted into the center comes out clean or with a few moist crumbs.
8. Allow the bread to cool in the pan for 10 minutes before transferring it to a wire rack to cool completely.
9. Once cooled, slice and enjoy this Vegan Pumpkin Chocolate Chip Bread as a deliciously spiced and chocolaty treat!

Gluten-Free Option:

- Substitute all-purpose flour with a gluten-free 1:1 flour blend.
- Add 1/2 teaspoon xanthan gum to the dry ingredients if the 1:1 flour doesn't have xanthan gum included.
- Ensure that the baking soda and baking powder are also gluten-free.

Jalapeño Cornbread

Yield: 1 loaf

Ingredients:

- 1 cup (120g) cornmeal
- 1 cup (125g) all-purpose flour
- 1 tablespoon (12g) baking powder
- 1/2 teaspoon (3g) baking soda
- 1/2 teaspoon (3g) salt
- 1 cup (240ml) non-dairy milk (such as almond or soy)
- 1 tablespoon (15ml) apple cider vinegar
- 1/4 cup (60ml) vegetable oil or melted coconut oil
- 1/4 cup (60ml) maple syrup or agave nectar
- 1 cup (150g) corn kernels (fresh, frozen, or canned)
- 2 medium jalapeños, seeded and finely chopped
- 1/4 cup pickled jalapeños, chopped (optional, for extra heat)

Directions:

1. Preheat the oven to 375°F (190°C). Grease an 8x8-inch (20x20cm) square baking dish.
2. In a medium bowl, whisk together the cornmeal, all-purpose flour, baking powder, baking soda, and salt.
3. In a separate bowl, combine the non-dairy milk and apple cider vinegar. Let it sit for a few minutes to curdle.
4. Add the vegetable oil and maple syrup (or agave nectar) to the curdled non-dairy milk mixture. Mix well.
5. Pour the wet ingredients into the bowl of dry ingredients. Stir until just combined.
6. Fold in the corn kernels, chopped jalapeños, and pickled jalapeños (if using).
7. Pour the batter into the prepared baking dish, spreading it evenly.
8. Bake in the preheated oven for 25-30 minutes or until a toothpick inserted into the center comes out clean or with a few moist crumbs.
9. Allow the cornbread to cool in the baking dish for 10 minutes before transferring it to a wire rack to cool completely.
10. Once cooled, slice and enjoy this Vegan Jalapeño Cornbread as a flavorful side dish or snack!

Gluten-Free Option:

- Substitute all-purpose flour with a gluten-free 1:1 flour blend.
- Add 1/4 teaspoon xanthan gum to the dry ingredients if the 1:1 flour doesn't have xanthan gum included.
- Ensure that the baking soda and baking powder are also gluten-free.

Artisan Dutch Oven Bread

Yield: 1 loaf

Ingredients:

- 4 cups (500g) bread flour
- 2 teaspoons (10g) salt
- 1 1/2 teaspoons (7g) active dry yeast
- 2 cups (480ml) lukewarm water

Directions:

1. In a large mixing bowl, combine the bread flour and salt.
2. In a small bowl, mix the active dry yeast with lukewarm water. Let it sit for a few minutes until the yeast is dissolved and becomes frothy.
3. Pour the yeast mixture into the flour mixture and stir with a wooden spoon until a shaggy dough forms.
4. Cover the bowl with a clean kitchen towel or plastic wrap and let the dough rest at room temperature for about 12-18 hours. This allows for fermentation and the development of flavor.
5. After the initial rise, the dough will be sticky and bubbly. Preheat your oven to 450°F (230°C). Place a Dutch oven (with lid) in the oven while it preheats.
6. While the oven is heating, transfer the sticky dough onto a floured surface. Gently fold the edges of the dough over onto itself, forming a rough ball.
7. Place the ball of dough on a piece of parchment paper, seam side down.
8. Once the oven is preheated, carefully remove the hot Dutch oven. Transfer the parchment paper with the dough into the Dutch oven.
9. Cover the Dutch oven with the lid and bake for 30 minutes.
10. After 30 minutes, remove the lid and bake for an additional 15-20 minutes or until the bread has a golden-brown crust.
11. Carefully remove the Dutch oven from the oven. Lift the bread out using the parchment paper and let it cool on a wire rack.
12. Allow the bread to cool completely before slicing.
13. Enjoy this simple and crusty Vegan Artisan Dutch Oven Bread with your favorite spreads or as a side to soups and stews!

Pumpernickel Sandwich Bread

Yield: 1 loaf

Ingredients:

- 2 1/2 cups (320g) dark rye flour
- 1 1/2 cups (190g) whole wheat flour
- 1 1/2 teaspoons (7g) salt
- 2 tablespoons (30g) molasses
- 2 tablespoons (30g) vegan butter, melted
- 1 1/2 teaspoons (7g) caraway seeds (optional)
- 1 1/2 teaspoons (7g) active dry yeast
- 1 1/2 cups (360ml) lukewarm water

Directions:

1. In a large mixing bowl, combine the dark rye flour, whole wheat flour, and salt.
2. In a small bowl, mix the active dry yeast with lukewarm water. Let it sit for a few minutes until the yeast is dissolved and becomes frothy.
3. Add the yeast mixture, molasses, melted vegan butter, and caraway seeds (if using) to the flour mixture. Stir until a sticky dough forms.
4. Transfer the dough to a floured surface and knead for about 5-7 minutes or until the dough becomes smooth and elastic. Add more flour if needed to prevent sticking.
5. Place the kneaded dough in a lightly oiled bowl, cover with a clean kitchen towel or plastic wrap, and let it rise in a warm place for about 1 to 1.5 hours, or until it has doubled in size.
6. Preheat the oven to 350°F (175°C). Grease a 9x5-inch (23x13cm) loaf pan.
7. Punch down the risen dough and shape it into a loaf. Place the shaped dough into the greased loaf pan.
8. Cover the pan with the kitchen towel or plastic wrap and let the dough rise for another 30-45 minutes.
9. Bake in the preheated oven for 30-40 minutes or until the bread sounds hollow when tapped on the bottom.
10. Allow the bread to cool in the pan for 10 minutes before transferring it to a wire rack to cool completely.
11. Once cooled, slice and enjoy this Vegan Pumpernickel Sandwich Bread for your favorite sandwiches or toasts!

Classic Sandwich Bread

Yield: 1 loaf

Ingredients:

- 4 cups (500g) all-purpose flour
- 1 tablespoon (12g) sugar
- 1 tablespoon (12g) active dry yeast
- 1 1/2 teaspoons (7g) salt
- 1 1/2 cups (360ml) warm water
- 2 tablespoons (30ml) vegetable oil
- Vegan butter for brushing (optional)

Directions:

1. In a small bowl, combine warm water and sugar. Stir until the sugar is dissolved. Sprinkle active dry yeast over the water and let it sit for 5-10 minutes until frothy.
2. In a large mixing bowl, combine the flour and salt.
3. Make a well in the center of the flour mixture and pour in the yeast mixture and vegetable oil.
4. Mix the ingredients until a dough forms.
5. Turn the dough onto a floured surface and knead for about 8-10 minutes, or until the dough becomes smooth and elastic. Add more flour if needed.
6. Place the dough in a lightly oiled bowl, cover with a clean kitchen towel or plastic wrap, and let it rise in a warm place for about 1-1.5 hours, or until it has doubled in size.
7. Punch down the risen dough and transfer it to a lightly floured surface.
8. Shape the dough into a rectangle and roll it up tightly, starting from the short side.
9. Place the rolled dough seam side down in a greased 9x5-inch (23x13cm) loaf pan.
10. Cover the pan with the kitchen towel or plastic wrap and let the dough rise for another 30-45 minutes.
11. Preheat the oven to 375°F (190°C).
12. Bake the bread in the preheated oven for 25-30 minutes or until the top is golden brown and the bread sounds hollow when tapped on the bottom.
13. Optional: Brush the top of the bread with melted vegan butter for a glossy finish.
14. Allow the bread to cool in the pan for 10 minutes before transferring it to a wire rack to cool completely.
15. Once cooled, slice and enjoy this Classic Sandwich Bread for your favorite sandwiches!

Burger Buns

Yield: 8 burger buns

Ingredients:

- 3 1/2 cups (440g) all-purpose flour
- 1 packet (2 1/4 teaspoons or 7g) active dry yeast
- 1 cup (240ml) warm water (about 110°F or 43°C)
- 1/4 cup (60ml) vegetable oil
- 2 tablespoons (25g) sugar
- 1 teaspoon (5g) salt
- Sesame seeds or poppy seeds for topping (optional)

Directions:

1. In a small bowl, combine warm water and sugar. Stir until the sugar is dissolved. Sprinkle active dry yeast over the water and let it sit for 5-10 minutes until frothy.
2. In a large mixing bowl, combine the flour and salt.
3. Make a well in the center of the flour mixture and pour in the yeast mixture and vegetable oil.
4. Mix the ingredients until a dough forms.
5. Turn the dough onto a floured surface and knead for about 8-10 minutes, or until the dough becomes smooth and elastic. Add more flour if needed.
6. Place the dough in a lightly oiled bowl, cover with a clean kitchen towel or plastic wrap, and let it rise in a warm place for about 1-1.5 hours, or until it has doubled in size.
7. Punch down the risen dough and transfer it to a lightly floured surface.
8. Divide the dough into 8 equal portions and shape each portion into a smooth ball.
9. Place the balls on a baking sheet lined with parchment paper, leaving space between each ball.
10. Cover the buns with the kitchen towel or plastic wrap and let them rise for another 30-45 minutes.
11. Preheat the oven to 375°F (190°C).
12. Optional: Brush the tops of the buns with water and sprinkle sesame seeds over them.
13. Bake the buns in the preheated oven for 15-20 minutes or until the tops are golden brown.
14. Allow the buns to cool on a wire rack.
15. Once cooled, slice and enjoy these Vegan Burger Buns for your favorite plant-based burgers!

Sourdough Starter

Ingredients:

- 1 cup (120g) whole wheat flour
- 1 cup (240ml) filtered water (chlorine-free)

Directions:

1. Day 1: Creating the Starter
2. In a glass or plastic container, mix 1 cup of whole wheat flour with 1 cup of filtered water until well combined.
3. Cover loosely with a cloth or plastic wrap and let it sit at room temperature (ideally around 70°F or 21°C) for 24 hours.
4. Day 2: First Feeding
5. You may or may not see signs of bubbling. Regardless, discard half of the mixture (about 1/2 cup).
6. Add 1 cup of whole wheat flour and 1 cup of filtered water. Mix well, cover loosely, and let it sit for another 24 hours.
7. Days 3-7: Daily Feedings
8. Continue discarding half of the mixture and feeding it with 1 cup of whole wheat flour and 1 cup of filtered water daily.
9. By day 3 or 4, you should notice increased bubbling and a slightly sour aroma. The starter is forming.
10. Transition to All-Purpose Flour
11. Once your starter is consistently doubling in size, you can transition to all-purpose flour for feedings.
12. Continue daily feedings with 1 cup of all-purpose flour and 1 cup of filtered water until the starter is consistently active and has a pleasant sour smell.
13. Maintaining the Starter
14. Once your starter is strong and active, you can switch to less frequent feedings (every 12-24 hours) and store it in the refrigerator between uses.
15. Before using it in a recipe, take it out, feed it, and let it come to room temperature.

Note:

Remember, creating a sourdough starter requires patience, and the environment and temperature can affect the process. It might take more or less time for your starter to become active. Be observant, and once it consistently doubles in size after feedings, you have a healthy, active sourdough starter ready to be used in your favorite bread recipes.

Sourdough Bread

Yield: 1 loaf

Ingredients:

- 1 cup (240g) active sourdough starter
- 1 1/2 cups (360ml) lukewarm water
- 4 cups (500g) bread flour
- 1 1/2 teaspoons (7g) salt

Directions:

1. Prepare the Dough: In a large mixing bowl, combine the active sourdough starter and lukewarm water.
2. Gradually add the bread flour and salt. Mix with a wooden spoon or your hands until a shaggy dough forms.
3. Kneading: Turn the dough onto a floured surface and knead for about 10-15 minutes, or until the dough becomes smooth and elastic. Add more flour as needed to prevent sticking.
4. First Rise: Place the kneaded dough in a lightly oiled bowl, cover it with a clean kitchen towel or plastic wrap, and let it rise at room temperature for 4-6 hours, or until it doubles in size. This is the bulk fermentation stage.
5. Shaping: Once the dough has doubled, turn it onto a floured surface and gently shape it into a round or oval shape.
6. Second Rise: Place the shaped dough on a floured surface, cover it, and let it rise for another 1-2 hours. This is the final proofing stage.
7. Preheat the Oven: About 30 minutes before baking, preheat your oven to 450°F (232°C). If you have a cast-iron Dutch oven, place it in the oven to preheat as well.
8. Baking: Optional: Slash the top of the dough with a sharp knife to allow for expansion.
9. Carefully transfer the dough into the preheated Dutch oven or onto a baking sheet lined with parchment paper.
10. If using a Dutch oven, cover with the lid. Bake for 20 minutes.
11. Remove the lid and continue baking for an additional 20-25 minutes, or until the crust is golden brown.
12. Cooling: Allow the bread to cool on a wire rack for at least 1 hour before slicing.

Garlic and Herb Bread

Yield: 1 loaf

Ingredients:

- 3 1/2 cups (440g) all-purpose flour
- 1 tablespoon (12g) sugar
- 1 tablespoon (12g) active dry yeast
- 1 1/2 teaspoons (7g) salt
- 1 cup (240ml) warm water (about 110°F or 43°C)
- 1/4 cup (60ml) olive oil
- 4 cloves garlic, minced
- 1 tablespoon (15g) dried mixed herbs (such as oregano, thyme, rosemary)
- Vegan butter for brushing (optional)

Directions:

1. Prepare the Dough: In a small bowl, combine warm water and sugar. Stir until the sugar is dissolved. Sprinkle active dry yeast over the water and let it sit for 5-10 minutes until frothy.
2. In a large mixing bowl, combine the flour and salt.
3. Make a well in the center of the flour mixture and pour in the yeast mixture and olive oil.
4. Mix the ingredients until a dough forms.
5. Kneading and Adding Flavors: Turn the dough onto a floured surface and knead for about 8-10 minutes, or until the dough becomes smooth and elastic. Add more flour if needed.
6. In the last few minutes of kneading, add the minced garlic and dried mixed herbs. Knead until the garlic and herbs are evenly distributed.
7. First Rise: Place the kneaded dough in a lightly oiled bowl, cover with a clean kitchen towel or plastic wrap, and let it rise in a warm place for about 1-1.5 hours, or until it has doubled in size.
8. Shaping and Second Rise: Once the dough has doubled, turn it onto a floured surface and shape it into a round or oval loaf.
9. Place the shaped dough on a baking sheet lined with parchment paper, cover it, and let it rise for another 30-45 minutes.
10. Preheat the Oven: About 30 minutes before baking, preheat your oven to 375°F (190°C).
11. Baking: Optional: Slash the top of the dough with a sharp knife.
12. Bake in the preheated oven for 25-30 minutes or until the top is golden brown.
13. Optional Finishing Touch: Brush the top of the bread with melted vegan butter for a glossy finish.
14. Cooling: Allow the bread to cool on a wire rack for at least 1 hour before slicing.

Ciabatta Bread

Yield: 2 loaves

Ingredients:

- 4 cups (500g) bread flour
- 1 1/2 teaspoons (7g) salt
- 1 packet (2 1/4 teaspoons or 7g) active dry yeast
- 2 cups (480ml) lukewarm water
- 2 tablespoons (30ml) olive oil
- Additional flour for dusting

Directions:

1. Activate the Yeast: In a small bowl, combine lukewarm water and yeast. Let it sit for 5-10 minutes until frothy.
2. Prepare the Dough: In a large mixing bowl, combine bread flour and salt. Make a well in the center.
3. Pour the activated yeast mixture and olive oil into the well.
4. Mixing and Kneading: Gradually incorporate the flour into the wet ingredients until a sticky dough forms.
5. Turn the dough onto a well-floured surface. Knead for about 10-15 minutes until the dough becomes smooth and elastic. Add more flour as needed to prevent sticking.
6. First Rise: Place the kneaded dough in a lightly oiled bowl. Cover it with a clean kitchen towel or plastic wrap.
7. Allow it to rise in a warm place for about 1.5 to 2 hours or until it doubles in size.
8. Shaping: Turn the risen dough onto a well-floured surface. Divide it into two equal portions.
9. Shape each portion into a rectangle, trying to maintain as much air as possible in the dough.
10. Second Rise: Place the shaped dough on a floured surface. Cover it with a kitchen towel and let it rise for another 1 to 1.5 hours.
11. Preheat the Oven: About 30 minutes before baking, preheat your oven to 450°F (232°C).
12. Baking: Transfer the risen dough rectangles to a baking sheet lined with parchment paper.
13. Bake in the preheated oven for 20-25 minutes or until the top is golden brown and the bread sounds hollow when tapped on the bottom.
14. Cooling: Allow the ciabatta loaves to cool on a wire rack for at least 30 minutes before slicing.

Orange Zucchini Bread

Yield: 1 loaf

Ingredients:

- 2 cups (250g) all-purpose flour
- 1 teaspoon (5g) baking powder
- 1/2 teaspoon (3g) baking soda
- 1/2 teaspoon (3g) salt
- 1 cup (200g) granulated sugar
- 1/2 cup (120ml) vegetable oil
- 1/4 cup (60ml) unsweetened applesauce
- 1/4 cup (60ml) fresh orange juice
- Zest of 1 orange
- 1 teaspoon (5ml) vanilla extract
- 1 1/2 cups (about 200g) grated zucchini (moisture squeezed out)
- 1/2 cup (60g) chopped walnuts or pecans (optional)
- Orange Glaze (Optional):
- 1 cup (120g) powdered sugar
- 2-3 tablespoons (30-45ml) fresh orange juice
- Orange zest for garnish (optional)

Directions:

1. Preheat your oven to 350°F (175°C). Grease and flour a 9x5-inch (23x13cm) loaf pan.
2. In a medium bowl, whisk together the all-purpose flour, baking powder, baking soda, and salt.
3. In a large bowl, combine the granulated sugar, vegetable oil, applesauce, fresh orange juice, orange zest, and vanilla extract. Mix well.
4. Gradually add the dry ingredients to the wet ingredients, mixing until just combined.
5. Fold in the grated zucchini and chopped nuts (if using) until evenly distributed in the batter.
6. Pour the batter into the prepared loaf pan, spreading it evenly.
7. Bake in the preheated oven for 55-65 minutes or until a toothpick inserted into the center comes out clean or with a few moist crumbs.
8. Allow the zucchini bread to cool in the pan for 10 minutes before transferring it to a wire rack to cool completely.
9. Prepare the Orange Glaze (Optional): In a small bowl, whisk together powdered sugar and fresh orange juice until you have a smooth glaze.
10. Once the bread has cooled, drizzle the orange glaze over the top. Optionally, garnish with additional orange zest for extra flavor.

Rosemary and Garlic Focaccia Bread

Yield: 1 large focaccia bread

Ingredients:

- For the Dough:
- 4 cups (500g) bread flour
- 2 teaspoons (8g) sugar
- 1 tablespoon (12g) active dry yeast
- 1 1/2 teaspoons (7g) salt
- 1 1/2 cups (360ml) lukewarm water
- 1/4 cup (60ml) olive oil
- For the Topping:
- 1/4 cup (60ml) olive oil
- 3 cloves garlic, minced
- Fresh rosemary sprigs
- Coarse sea salt for sprinkling

Directions:

1. **Activate the Yeast:** In a small bowl, combine lukewarm water and sugar. Stir until the sugar is dissolved. Sprinkle active dry yeast over the water and let it sit for 5-10 minutes until frothy.
2. **Prepare the Dough:** In a large mixing bowl, combine bread flour and salt. Make a well in the center.
3. Pour the activated yeast mixture and olive oil into the well.
4. Gradually incorporate the flour into the wet ingredients until a dough forms.
5. **Kneading:** Turn the dough onto a floured surface. Knead for about 10-15 minutes until the dough becomes smooth and elastic. Add more flour as needed.
6. **First Rise:** Place the kneaded dough in a lightly oiled bowl. Cover it with a clean kitchen towel or plastic wrap.
7. Allow it to rise in a warm place for about 1 to 1.5 hours or until it has doubled in size.
8. **Shaping:** Turn the risen dough onto a floured surface. Press it into a large rectangle or shape of your choice.
9. Transfer the shaped dough to a parchment-lined baking sheet.
10. **Second Rise:** Cover the shaped dough with a kitchen towel and let it rise for another 30-45 minutes.
11. **Preheat the Oven:** About 30 minutes before baking, preheat your oven to 425°F (220°C).
12. **Topping:** In a small bowl, mix together olive oil and minced garlic.
13. Using your fingertips, make dimples all over the surface of the risen dough.
14. Brush the olive oil and garlic mixture over the dough.
15. Place fresh rosemary sprigs into the dimples.
16. **Baking:** Bake in the preheated oven for 20-25 minutes or until the top is golden brown.
17. **Finishing:** While the focaccia is still hot, sprinkle coarse sea salt over the top.
18. **Cooling:** Allow the focaccia to cool on a wire rack for at least 15 minutes before slicing.

Spinach Tomato Babka

Yield: 1 Babka

Ingredients:

- For the Dough:
- 4 cups (500g) all-purpose flour
- 1/4 cup (50g) granulated sugar
- 1 tablespoon (12g) active dry yeast
- 1 teaspoon (5g) salt
- 1 cup (240ml) plant-based milk, lukewarm
- 1/2 cup (120g) vegan butter, melted
- For the Filling:
- 1 cup (about 150g) fresh spinach, finely chopped
- 1 cup (about 150g) cherry tomatoes, quartered
- 1/2 cup (120g) vegan cream cheese
- 2 cloves garlic, minced
- 2 tablespoons (30ml) olive oil
- Salt and pepper to taste
- For Assembly:
- Olive oil for brushing
- Flour for dusting

Directions:

1. **Activate the Yeast:** In a small bowl, combine lukewarm plant-based milk and sugar. Stir until the sugar is dissolved. Sprinkle active dry yeast over the milk and let it sit for 5-10 minutes until frothy.
2. **Prepare the Dough:** In a large mixing bowl, combine all-purpose flour and salt.
3. Make a well in the center and pour in the activated yeast mixture and melted vegan butter.
4. Mix until a dough forms. Knead the dough on a floured surface for about 5-8 minutes until it becomes smooth and elastic.
5. **First Rise:** Place the kneaded dough in a lightly oiled bowl. Cover it with a clean kitchen towel or plastic wrap.
6. Allow it to rise in a warm place for about 1 to 1.5 hours or until it has doubled in size.
7. **Prepare the Filling:** In a pan, sauté chopped spinach and minced garlic in olive oil until the spinach is wilted. Season with salt and pepper.
8. Remove from heat and let it cool.
9. Mix the cooled spinach with quartered cherry tomatoes and vegan cream cheese.
10. **Assemble the Babka:** Preheat the oven to 350°F (175°C).
11. Roll out the risen dough on a floured surface into a large rectangle.
12. Spread the spinach-tomato-cream cheese filling evenly over the dough.
13. Roll the dough tightly from one end to form a log.
14. **Shape the Babka:** Using a sharp knife, slice the log in half lengthwise, exposing the layers.
15. Twist the two pieces together, keeping the cut sides facing up.
16. Place the twisted dough into a greased and floured loaf pan.
17. **Second Rise:** Cover the pan with a kitchen towel and let it rise for another 30-45 minutes.
18. **Baking:** Brush the top of the risen babka with olive oil.
19. Bake in the preheated oven for 30-35 minutes or until the top is golden brown.
20. **Cooling:** Allow the babka to cool in the pan for 15-20 minutes before transferring it to a wire rack.

Garlic Herb Naan

Yield: 6 Naan

Ingredients:

- For the Naan Dough:
- 2 cups (250g) all-purpose flour
- 1 teaspoon (5g) sugar
- 1 teaspoon (5g) active dry yeast
- 1/2 teaspoon (3g) salt
- 3/4 cup (180ml) warm plant-based milk
- 2 tablespoons (30ml) olive oil
- For the Garlic Herb Butter:
- 1/4 cup (60g) vegan butter, melted
- 3 cloves garlic, minced
- 1 tablespoon (15g) fresh parsley, finely chopped
- 1 tablespoon (15g) fresh cilantro, finely chopped (optional)
- Salt to taste

Directions:

1. Activate the Yeast: In a small bowl, combine warm plant-based milk and sugar. Stir until the sugar is dissolved. Sprinkle active dry yeast over the milk and let it sit for 5-10 minutes until frothy.
2. Prepare the Naan Dough: In a large mixing bowl, combine all-purpose flour and salt.
3. Make a well in the center and pour in the activated yeast mixture and olive oil.
4. Mix until a soft dough forms. Knead the dough on a floured surface for about 5 minutes until it becomes smooth and elastic.
5. Place the kneaded dough in a lightly oiled bowl. Cover it with a kitchen towel or plastic wrap and let it rise in a warm place for 1-2 hours or until it doubles in size.
6. Preheat the Oven: Preheat your oven to the highest setting (usually around 500°F or 260°C). If you have a pizza stone, place it in the oven to heat.
7. Prepare the Garlic Herb Butter: In a small bowl, mix together melted vegan butter, minced garlic, chopped parsley, and cilantro (if using). Add salt to taste.
8. Shape and Cook the Naan: Divide the risen dough into 6 equal portions.
9. Roll out each portion into an oval or round shape, about 1/4 inch thick.
10. If using a pizza stone, transfer the rolled-out naan directly onto the stone. Alternatively, use a baking sheet lined with parchment paper.
11. Bake for 5-7 minutes or until the naan puffs up and the edges turn golden brown.
12. Garlic Herb Finish: Brush the hot naan with the prepared garlic herb butter immediately after removing them from the oven.

Spiced Christmas Bread

Yield: 1 loaf

Ingredients:

- For the Dough:
- 4 cups (500g) all-purpose flour
- 1/2 cup (100g) granulated sugar
- 1 tablespoon (12g) active dry yeast
- 1 teaspoon (5g) salt
- 1 1/2 teaspoons (4g) ground cinnamon
- 1/2 teaspoon (1g) ground nutmeg
- 1/4 teaspoon (1g) ground cloves
- 1 1/4 cups (300ml) warm plant-based milk
- 1/2 cup (120g) vegan butter, melted
- For the Filling:
- 1/2 cup (100g) brown sugar
- 2 teaspoons (5g) ground cinnamon
- 1/2 cup (120g) chopped nuts (walnuts, pecans, or almonds)
- 1/2 cup (80g) chopped dried fruits (raisins, cranberries, or apricots)
- For the Glaze:
- 1 cup (120g) powdered sugar
- 2 tablespoons (30ml) plant-based milk
- 1/2 teaspoon (2.5ml) vanilla extract

Directions:

1. Activate the Yeast: In a small bowl, combine warm plant-based milk and 1 tablespoon of sugar. Stir until the sugar is dissolved. Sprinkle active dry yeast over the milk and let it sit for 5-10 minutes until frothy.
2. Prepare the Dough: In a large mixing bowl, combine all-purpose flour, remaining sugar, salt, ground cinnamon, ground nutmeg, and ground cloves.
3. Make a well in the center and pour in the activated yeast mixture and melted vegan butter.
4. Mix until a soft dough forms. Knead the dough on a floured surface for about 8-10 minutes until it becomes smooth and elastic.
5. Place the kneaded dough in a lightly oiled bowl. Cover it with a kitchen towel or plastic wrap and let it rise in a warm place for 1-2 hours or until it has doubled in size.
6. Prepare the Filling: In a small bowl, mix together brown sugar, ground cinnamon, chopped nuts, and dried fruits.
7. Assemble the Christmas Bread: Roll out the risen dough on a floured surface into a large rectangle.
8. Spread the filling mixture evenly over the dough.
9. Roll the dough tightly from one end to form a log.
10. Shape the Bread: Place the rolled dough in a greased and floured loaf pan. You can also shape it into a wreath for a festive touch.
11. Second Rise: Cover the pan with a kitchen towel and let it rise for another 30-45 minutes.
12. Preheat the Oven: Preheat your oven to 350°F (175°C).
13. Baking: Bake in the preheated oven for 30-35 minutes or until the top is golden brown.
14. Prepare the Glaze: In a small bowl, whisk together powdered sugar, plant-based milk, and vanilla extract until you have a smooth glaze.
15. Glaze the Bread: Once the Christmas bread is out of the oven, drizzle the glaze over the top while it's still warm.
16. Cooling: Allow the bread to cool in the pan for 15-20 minutes before transferring it to a wire rack.

Butterscotch Bread Pudding

Yield: 8 servings

Ingredients:

- For the Bread Pudding:
- 6 cups (about 300g) day-old bread, cubed
- 1 1/2 cups (360ml) plant-based milk (such as almond or soy)
- 1/2 cup (120g) brown sugar
- 1/2 cup (120g) vegan butterscotch chips
- 1/4 cup (30g) cornstarch
- 1 teaspoon (5ml) vanilla extract
- 1/2 teaspoon (3g) ground cinnamon
- 1/4 teaspoon (2g) salt
- Vegan whipped cream or ice cream for serving (optional)
- For the Butterscotch Sauce:
- 1/2 cup (120g) vegan butter
- 1 cup (200g) brown sugar
- 1/2 cup (120ml) plant-based cream
- 1/4 teaspoon (2g) salt
- 1 teaspoon (5ml) vanilla extract

Directions:

1. Preheat your oven to 350°F (175°C). Grease a baking dish.
2. In a large bowl, combine the cubed bread and butterscotch chips.
3. In a blender or food processor, combine plant-based milk, brown sugar, cornstarch, vanilla extract, ground cinnamon, and salt. Blend until smooth.
4. Pour the blended mixture over the bread and butterscotch chips. Gently stir to coat the bread evenly.
5. Let the mixture sit for 15-20 minutes to allow the bread to absorb the custard.
6. Transfer to Baking Dish: Pour the soaked bread mixture into the prepared baking dish, spreading it evenly.
7. Bake: Bake in the preheated oven for 35-40 minutes or until the top is golden brown, and the center is set.
8. Prepare the Butterscotch Sauce: In a saucepan, melt vegan butter over medium heat. Add brown sugar and plant-based cream, stirring constantly.
9. Bring the mixture to a gentle boil, then reduce the heat and simmer for 2-3 minutes until the sauce thickens.
10. Remove from heat and stir in salt and vanilla extract.
11. Once the bread pudding is out of the oven, drizzle the warm butterscotch sauce over the top.
12. Allow the pudding to cool for a few minutes before serving.
13. Serve with a dollop of vegan whipped cream or a scoop of dairy-free ice cream for an extra indulgent treat.

French Toast Bread Pudding

Yield: 6 servings

Ingredients:

- For the Bread Pudding:
- 6 cups (about 300g) day-old bread, cubed
- 1 1/2 cups (360ml) plant-based milk (such as almond or soy)
- 1/2 cup (120g) granulated sugar
- 4 tablespoons (60ml) maple syrup
- 1 teaspoon (5ml) vanilla extract
- 1/2 teaspoon (3g) ground cinnamon
- 1/4 teaspoon (2g) ground nutmeg
- Pinch of salt
- Vegan butter for greasing the baking dish
- For the Maple Glaze:
- 1/2 cup (120ml) maple syrup
- 1/4 cup (30g) powdered sugar
- Optional Toppings:
- Fresh berries
- Vegan whipped cream
- Chopped nuts

Directions:

1. Preheat your oven to 350°F (175°C). Grease a baking dish with vegan butter.
2. In a large bowl, combine the cubed bread.
3. In a separate bowl, whisk together plant-based milk, granulated sugar, maple syrup, vanilla extract, ground cinnamon, ground nutmeg, and a pinch of salt.
4. Pour the wet mixture over the bread cubes, ensuring they are well coated. Allow the bread to soak for 15-20 minutes.
5. Spread the soaked bread cubes evenly in the prepared baking dish.
6. Bake in the preheated oven for 30-35 minutes or until the top is golden brown and the center is set.
7. In a small saucepan, heat maple syrup over low-medium heat until warm. Whisk in powdered sugar until the glaze is smooth.
8. Drizzle the warm maple glaze over the top of the bread pudding.
9. Allow the French Toast Bread Pudding to cool for a few minutes before serving.
10. Optional: Garnish with fresh berries, a dollop of vegan whipped cream, or chopped nuts for added flavor and texture.

Hot Buttered Rum Bread Pudding

Yield: 8 servings

Ingredients:

- For the Bread Pudding:
- 6 cups (about 300g) day-old bread, cubed
- 2 cups (480ml) plant-based milk (such as almond or soy)
- 1/2 cup (120g) brown sugar
- 1/4 cup (60g) vegan butter, melted
- 3 tablespoons (45ml) dark rum
- 1 teaspoon (5ml) vanilla extract
- 1/2 teaspoon (3g) ground cinnamon
- 1/4 teaspoon (2g) ground nutmeg
- Pinch of salt
- Vegan butter for greasing the baking dish
- For the Rum Sauce:
- 1/2 cup (120g) brown sugar
- 1/4 cup (60g) vegan butter
- 2 tablespoons (30ml) dark rum
- 1/4 cup (60ml) plant-based cream
- Optional Toppings:
- Vegan whipped cream
- Chopped nuts
- Cinnamon for dusting

Directions:

1. Preheat your oven to 350°F (175°C). Grease a baking dish with vegan butter.
2. In a large bowl, combine the cubed bread.
3. In a separate bowl, whisk together plant-based milk, brown sugar, melted vegan butter, dark rum, vanilla extract, ground cinnamon, ground nutmeg, and a pinch of salt.
4. Pour the wet mixture over the bread cubes, ensuring they are well coated. Allow the bread to soak for 15-20 minutes.
5. Spread the soaked bread cubes evenly in the prepared baking dish.
6. Bake in the preheated oven for 35-40 minutes or until the top is golden brown and the center is set.
7. In a saucepan, combine brown sugar, vegan butter, dark rum, and plant-based cream for the rum sauce. Heat over medium heat, stirring constantly until the sugar is dissolved and the sauce is smooth.
8. Once the bread pudding is out of the oven, drizzle the warm rum sauce over the top.
9. Allow the Hot Buttered Rum Bread Pudding to cool for a few minutes before serving.
10. Optional: Garnish with vegan whipped cream, chopped nuts, and a dusting of cinnamon for an extra touch of indulgence.

CHAPTER 5

Cakes & Cupcakes

Raspberry Swirl Cheesecake

Yield: 10 servings

Ingredients:

- For the Crust:
- 1 1/2 cups (150g) graham cracker crumbs
- 1/4 cup (60g) vegan butter, melted
- 2 tablespoons (30g) granulated sugar
- For the Cheesecake Filling:
- 2 cups (480g) vegan cream cheese, softened
- 1 cup (200g) granulated sugar
- 1/4 cup (30g) all-purpose flour
- 1/2 cup (120ml) coconut cream
- 1 teaspoon (5ml) vanilla extract
- 1/4 teaspoon (1.25g) salt
- 3 tablespoons (45ml) lemon juice
- For the Raspberry Swirl:
- 1 cup (125g) fresh or frozen raspberries
- 2 tablespoons (30g) granulated sugar
- 1 tablespoon (15ml) lemon juice

Directions:

1. Preheat your oven to 325°F (163°C). Grease a 9-inch (23cm) springform pan.
2. Prepare the Crust: In a bowl, mix graham cracker crumbs, melted vegan butter, and granulated sugar until well combined.
3. Press the mixture into the bottom of the prepared springform pan to form an even crust.
4. Prepare the Raspberry Swirl: In a saucepan over medium heat, combine raspberries, granulated sugar, and lemon juice.
5. Cook for 5-7 minutes, stirring occasionally, until the raspberries break down and the mixture thickens.
6. Strain the mixture through a fine mesh sieve to remove seeds, if desired. Set aside.
7. Prepare the Cheesecake Filling: In a large bowl, beat the vegan cream cheese until smooth.
8. Add granulated sugar and flour, and beat until well combined.
9. Mix in coconut cream, vanilla extract, salt, and lemon juice until the batter is smooth.
10. Assemble and Bake: Pour the cheesecake filling over the prepared crust in the springform pan.
11. Drop spoonfuls of the raspberry swirl mixture on top.
12. Use a knife or skewer to create a marbled effect by swirling the raspberry mixture into the cheesecake batter.
13. Bake in the preheated oven for 45-50 minutes or until the edges are set, and the center is slightly jiggly.
14. Cooling and Chilling: Allow the cheesecake to cool in the pan on a wire rack for 1 hour.
15. Refrigerate for at least 4 hours or preferably overnight to set.
16. Serve: Run a knife around the edges of the pan before releasing the springform sides.
17. Slice and serve chilled.
18. Optional: Garnish with additional fresh raspberries or a dollop of vegan whipped cream when serving.

Pumpkin Spice Sheet Cake

Yield: 12 servings

Ingredients:

- For the Cake:
- 2 cups (250g) all-purpose flour
- 1 1/2 teaspoons (7.5g) baking powder
- 1 teaspoon (5g) baking soda
- 1/2 teaspoon (3g) salt
- 2 teaspoons (4g) ground cinnamon
- 1/2 teaspoon (1g) ground nutmeg
- 1/2 teaspoon (1g) ground ginger
- 1/4 teaspoon (0.5g) ground cloves
- 1 cup (200g) granulated sugar
- 1 cup (240ml) pumpkin puree
- 1/2 cup (120ml) vegetable oil
- 1/2 cup (120ml) plant-based milk (such as almond or soy)
- 2 teaspoons (10ml) vanilla extract
- For the Cream Cheese Frosting:
- 1/2 cup (115g) vegan cream cheese, softened
- 1/4 cup (60g) vegan butter, softened
- 2 cups (250g) powdered sugar
- 1 teaspoon (5ml) vanilla extract

Directions:

1. Preheat your oven to 350°F (175°C). Grease and flour a 9x13-inch (23x33cm) baking pan.
2. Prepare the Cake: In a medium bowl, whisk together flour, baking powder, baking soda, salt, cinnamon, nutmeg, ginger, and cloves.
3. In a large bowl, whisk together sugar, pumpkin puree, vegetable oil, plant-based milk, and vanilla extract until well combined.
4. Gradually add the dry ingredients to the wet ingredients, mixing until just combined. Do not overmix.
5. Pour the batter into the prepared baking pan, spreading it evenly.
6. Bake in the preheated oven for 25-30 minutes or until a toothpick inserted into the center comes out clean.
7. Prepare the Cream Cheese Frosting: In a mixing bowl, beat the vegan cream cheese and butter until smooth and creamy.
8. Gradually add powdered sugar, beating until well combined.
9. Mix in vanilla extract.
10. Once the cake has cooled, spread the cream cheese frosting over the top.
11. Optional: Sprinkle a dash of ground cinnamon or pumpkin spice over the frosting for an extra touch of flavor.

Berry Chantilly Cake

Yield: 12 servings

Ingredients:

- For the Cake:
- 2 1/2 cups (315g) all-purpose flour
- 2 1/2 teaspoons (12.5g) baking powder
- 1/2 teaspoon (3g) salt
- 1 cup (240ml) plant-based milk (such as almond or soy)
- 1 teaspoon (5ml) vanilla extract
- 1 cup (200g) granulated sugar
- 1/2 cup (120ml) vegetable oil
- 1/2 cup (120ml) unsweetened applesauce
- For the Berry Filling:
- 2 cups (300g) mixed berries (strawberries, blueberries, raspberries)
- 1/4 cup (50g) granulated sugar
- 1 tablespoon (15ml) lemon juice
- For the Chantilly Cream:
- 2 cups (480ml) coconut cream (chilled)
- 1/2 cup (60g) powdered sugar
- 1 teaspoon (5ml) vanilla extract
- Additional Toppings:
- Fresh berries for garnish

Directions:

1. Preheat your oven to 350°F (175°C). Grease and flour two 9-inch (23cm) round cake pans.
2. Prepare the Cake: In a medium bowl, whisk together flour, baking powder, and salt.
3. In a separate bowl, mix plant-based milk and vanilla extract.
4. In a large bowl, beat together granulated sugar, vegetable oil, and applesauce until well combined.
5. Gradually add the dry ingredients to the wet ingredients, alternating with the milk mixture, beginning and ending with the dry ingredients. Mix until just combined.
6. Divide the batter evenly between the prepared cake pans and smooth the tops.
7. Bake in the preheated oven for 25-30 minutes or until a toothpick inserted into the center comes out clean.
8. Prepare the Berry Filling: In a saucepan, combine mixed berries, granulated sugar, and lemon juice.
9. Cook over medium heat for 5-7 minutes, or until the berries break down and the mixture thickens. Remove from heat and let it cool.
10. Prepare the Chantilly Cream: In a mixing bowl, beat the chilled coconut cream, powdered sugar, and vanilla extract until stiff peaks form.
11. Assemble the Cake: Once the cakes are completely cooled, place one layer on a serving plate.
12. Spread a layer of the Chantilly cream on top of the first layer.
13. Spoon the berry filling over the Chantilly cream.
14. Place the second cake layer on top and repeat with Chantilly cream and berry filling.
15. Garnish with Fresh Berries: Decorate the top of the cake with fresh berries.
16. Refrigerate the cake for at least 2 hours before serving to allow the flavors to meld.

Black Forest Cake

Yield: 12 servings

Ingredients:

- For the Chocolate Cake:
- 2 cups (250g) all-purpose flour
- 1 1/2 cups (300g) granulated sugar
- 3/4 cup (75g) unsweetened cocoa powder
- 2 teaspoons (10g) baking powder
- 1 1/2 teaspoons (7.5g) baking soda
- 1 teaspoon (5g) salt
- 1 3/4 cups (420ml) plant-based milk (such as almond or soy)
- 1/2 cup (120ml) vegetable oil
- 2 teaspoons (10ml) vanilla extract
- 2 tablespoons (30ml) apple cider vinegar
- For the Cherry Filling:
- 2 cups (300g) pitted cherries, halved
- 1/4 cup (50g) granulated sugar
- 1 tablespoon (15ml) lemon juice
- 2 tablespoons (16g) cornstarch mixed with 2 tablespoons water (cornstarch slurry)
- For the Coconut Whipped Cream:
- 2 cans (800ml) coconut cream, chilled overnight
- 1/2 cup (60g) powdered sugar
- 1 teaspoon (5ml) vanilla extract
- For Garnish:
- Vegan chocolate shavings or grated chocolate
- Additional fresh cherries

Directions:

1. Preheat your oven to 350°F (175°C). Grease and flour two 9-inch (23cm) round cake pans.
2. Prepare the Chocolate Cake: In a large bowl, whisk together flour, sugar, cocoa powder, baking powder, baking soda, and salt.
3. In a separate bowl, whisk together plant-based milk, vegetable oil, vanilla extract, and apple cider vinegar.
4. Pour the wet ingredients into the dry ingredients and mix until just combined.
5. Divide the batter evenly between the prepared cake pans and smooth the tops.
6. Bake in the preheated oven for 25-30 minutes or until a toothpick inserted into the center comes out clean.
7. Prepare the Cherry Filling: In a saucepan, combine halved cherries, granulated sugar, and lemon juice. Cook over medium heat until the cherries release their juices.
8. Stir in the cornstarch slurry and continue cooking until the mixture thickens. Remove from heat and let it cool.
9. Prepare the Coconut Whipped Cream: Open the chilled coconut cream cans without shaking and scoop out the thick cream, leaving behind the liquid.
10. In a mixing bowl, whip the coconut cream, powdered sugar, and vanilla extract until stiff peaks form.
11. Assemble the Black Forest Cake: Once the cakes are completely cooled, place one layer on a serving plate.
12. Spread a layer of coconut whipped cream over the first layer.
13. Spoon the cherry filling over the whipped cream.
14. Place the second cake layer on top and repeat with whipped cream and cherry filling.
15. Garnish with Chocolate and Cherries: Decorate the top and sides of the cake with vegan chocolate shavings or grated chocolate.
16. Garnish with additional fresh cherries.
17. Refrigerate the cake for at least 2 hours before serving to allow the flavors to meld.

Lemon Olive Oil Cake

Yield: 10 servings

Ingredients:

- For the Cake:
- 2 cups (250g) all-purpose flour
- 1 cup (200g) granulated sugar
- 1 teaspoon (5g) baking powder
- 1/2 teaspoon (2.5g) baking soda
- 1/4 teaspoon (1g) salt
- 1 cup (240ml) plant-based milk (such as almond or soy)
- 1/2 cup (120ml) extra virgin olive oil
- 1/4 cup (60ml) lemon juice
- Zest of 2 lemons
- 1 teaspoon (5ml) vanilla extract
- For the Lemon Glaze:
- 1 cup (120g) powdered sugar
- 2 tablespoons (30ml) lemon juice
- Zest of 1 lemon
- For Garnish:
- Sliced lemon rounds
- Fresh mint leaves

Gluten-Free Option:

- Substitute all-purpose flour with a gluten-free 1:1 flour blend.
- Add 1/2 teaspoon xanthan gum to the dry ingredients if the 1:1 flour doesn't have xanthan gum included.
- Ensure that the baking powder and baking soda are also gluten-free.

Directions:

1. Preheat your oven to 350°F (175°C). Grease and flour a 9-inch (23cm) round cake pan.
2. Prepare the Cake: In a large bowl, whisk together flour, sugar, baking powder, baking soda, and salt.
3. In a separate bowl, whisk together plant-based milk, olive oil, lemon juice, lemon zest, and vanilla extract.
4. Pour the wet ingredients into the dry ingredients and mix until just combined.
5. Pour the batter into the prepared cake pan, spreading it evenly.
6. Bake in the preheated oven for 30-35 minutes or until a toothpick inserted into the center comes out clean.
7. Prepare the Lemon Glaze: In a bowl, whisk together powdered sugar, lemon juice, and lemon zest until smooth.
8. Once the cake is completely cooled, drizzle the lemon glaze over the top.
9. Garnish with Sliced Lemons and Mint:
10. Decorate the top of the cake with sliced lemon rounds and fresh mint leaves.

Blueberry Bergamot Cupcakes

Yield: 12 cupcakes

Ingredients:

- For the Cupcakes:
- 1 1/2 cups (180g) all-purpose flour
- 1 1/2 teaspoons (8g) baking powder
- 1/2 teaspoon (3g) baking soda
- 1/4 teaspoon (1g) salt
- 1/2 cup (120ml) plant-based milk (such as almond or soy)
- 1/2 cup (120ml) olive oil
- 2 Earl Grey tea bags
- 3/4 cup (150g) granulated sugar
- 1 teaspoon (5ml) vanilla extract
- Zest of 1 lemon
- 1 cup (150g) fresh blueberries
- For the Earl Grey Frosting:
- 1/2 cup (120g) vegan butter, softened
- 2 cups (250g) powdered sugar
- 2 tablespoons (30ml) strong brewed Earl Grey tea, cooled
- Zest of 1 lemon
- For Garnish:
- Fresh blueberries
- Lemon zest

Gluten-Free Option:

- Substitute all-purpose flour with a gluten-free 1:1 flour blend.
- Add 1/2 teaspoon xanthan gum to the dry ingredients if the 1:1 flour doesn't have xanthan gum included.
- Ensure that the baking powder and baking soda are also gluten-free.

Directions:

1. Preheat your oven to 350°F (175°C). Line a muffin tin with cupcake liners.
2. Prepare the Cupcakes: Heat the plant-based milk until warm but not boiling. Steep the Earl Grey tea bags in the warm milk for 10 minutes, then remove the tea bags.
3. In a bowl, whisk together flour, baking powder, baking soda, and salt.
4. In another bowl, combine the olive oil, Earl Grey-infused milk, granulated sugar, vanilla extract, and lemon zest.
5. Add the wet ingredients to the dry ingredients and mix until just combined.
6. Gently fold in the fresh blueberries.
7. Divide the batter evenly among the cupcake liners.
8. Bake in the preheated oven for 18-20 minutes or until a toothpick inserted into the center comes out clean.
9. Prepare the Earl Grey Frosting: In a mixing bowl, beat vegan butter until creamy.
10. Gradually add powdered sugar, brewed Earl Grey tea, and lemon zest, beating until smooth and fluffy.
11. Once the cupcakes are completely cooled, frost them with the Earl Grey frosting.
12. Garnish with Fresh Blueberries and Lemon Zest: Top each cupcake with fresh blueberries and a sprinkle of lemon zest.

Strawberry Champagne Cupcakes

Yield: 12 cupcakes

Ingredients:

- For the Cupcakes:
- 1 1/2 cups (180g) all-purpose flour
- 1 1/2 teaspoons (8g) baking powder
- 1/2 teaspoon (3g) baking soda
- 1/4 teaspoon (1g) salt
- 1/2 cup (120ml) plant-based milk (such as almond or soy)
- 1/2 cup (120ml) olive oil
- 1 cup (200g) granulated sugar
- 1 teaspoon (5ml) vanilla extract
- 1/2 cup (120ml) champagne or sparkling wine
- 1 cup (150g) fresh strawberries, chopped
- For the Strawberry Champagne Frosting:
- 1/2 cup (120g) vegan butter, softened
- 2 cups (250g) powdered sugar
- 2 tablespoons (30ml) champagne or sparkling wine
- 1/2 cup (75g) fresh strawberries, pureed
- For Garnish:
- Fresh strawberries, sliced
- Edible flowers (optional)

Directions:

1. Preheat your oven to 350°F (175°C). Line a muffin tin with cupcake liners.
2. Prepare the Cupcakes: In a bowl, whisk together flour, baking powder, baking soda, and salt.
3. In another bowl, combine the plant-based milk, olive oil, granulated sugar, vanilla extract, and champagne.
4. Add the wet ingredients to the dry ingredients and mix until just combined.
5. Gently fold in the chopped strawberries.
6. Divide the batter evenly among the cupcake liners.
7. Bake in the preheated oven for 18-20 minutes or until a toothpick inserted into the center comes out clean.
8. Prepare the Strawberry Champagne Frosting: In a mixing bowl, beat vegan butter until creamy.
9. Gradually add powdered sugar, champagne, and pureed strawberries, beating until smooth and fluffy.
10. Once the cupcakes are completely cooled, frost them with the Strawberry Champagne frosting.
11. Garnish with Fresh Strawberries and Edible Flowers: Top each cupcake with sliced fresh strawberries and, if desired, edible flowers for a decorative touch.

Gluten-Free Option:

- Substitute all-purpose flour with a gluten-free 1:1 flour blend.
- Add 1/2 teaspoon xanthan gum to the dry ingredients if the 1:1 flour doesn't have xanthan gum included.
- Ensure that the baking powder and baking soda are also gluten-free.

Apple Cinnamon Bundt Cake

Yield: 12 servings

Ingredients:

- For the Cake:
- 3 cups (360g) all-purpose flour
- 2 teaspoons (10g) baking powder
- 1 teaspoon (5g) baking soda
- 1/2 teaspoon (3g) salt
- 1 1/2 teaspoons (3g) ground cinnamon
- 1/2 cup (120ml) vegetable oil
- 1 cup (240ml) unsweetened applesauce
- 1 cup (200g) granulated sugar
- 1/2 cup (120ml) maple syrup
- 1/2 cup (120ml) plant-based milk (such as almond or soy)
- 1 teaspoon (5ml) vanilla extract
- 2 cups (200g) apples, peeled and finely chopped
- For the Cinnamon Glaze:
- 1 cup (120g) powdered sugar
- 2 tablespoons (30ml) plant-based milk
- 1/2 teaspoon (3g) ground cinnamon
- 1/2 teaspoon (3ml) vanilla extract

Gluten-Free Option:

- Substitute all-purpose flour with a gluten-free 1:1 flour blend.
- Add 3/4 teaspoon xanthan gum to the dry ingredients if the 1:1 flour doesn't have xanthan gum included.
- Ensure that the baking powder and baking soda are also gluten-free.

Directions:

1. Preheat your oven to 350°F (175°C). Grease and flour a bundt cake pan.
2. Prepare the Cake: In a large bowl, whisk together flour, baking powder, baking soda, salt, and ground cinnamon.
3. In a separate bowl, combine vegetable oil, applesauce, granulated sugar, maple syrup, plant-based milk, and vanilla extract.
4. Add the wet ingredients to the dry ingredients and mix until just combined.
5. Fold in the chopped apples.
6. Pour the batter into the prepared bundt cake pan, spreading it evenly.
7. Bake in the preheated oven for 45-50 minutes or until a toothpick inserted into the center comes out clean.
8. Prepare the Cinnamon Glaze: In a bowl, whisk together powdered sugar, plant-based milk, ground cinnamon, and vanilla extract until smooth.
9. Once the cake is completely cooled, drizzle the cinnamon glaze over the top.

Cinnamon Coffee Cake

Yield: 12 servings

Ingredients:

- For the Cake:
- 2 cups (250g) all-purpose flour
- 1 cup (200g) granulated sugar
- 1/2 cup (120ml) vegetable oil
- 1 cup (240ml) plant-based milk (such as almond or soy)
- 1 tablespoon (15ml) apple cider vinegar
- 1 teaspoon (5g) baking powder
- 1/2 teaspoon (3g) baking soda
- 1/4 teaspoon (1g) salt
- For the Cinnamon Swirl:
- 1/2 cup (100g) brown sugar, packed
- 2 teaspoons (5g) ground cinnamon
- For the Streusel Topping:
- 1/2 cup (100g) brown sugar, packed
- 1/2 cup (60g) all-purpose flour
- 2 teaspoons (5g) ground cinnamon
- 1/4 cup (60g) vegan butter, melted
- For the Glaze:
- 1 cup (120g) powdered sugar
- 2 tablespoons (30ml) plant-based milk
- 1/2 teaspoon (3ml) vanilla extract

Directions:

1. Preheat your oven to 350°F (175°C). Grease a 9x13-inch baking pan.
2. Prepare the Cake: In a large bowl, whisk together flour, sugar, baking powder, baking soda, and salt.
3. In a separate bowl, mix together vegetable oil, plant-based milk, and apple cider vinegar.
4. Pour the wet ingredients into the dry ingredients and stir until just combined. Avoid overmixing.
5. Prepare the Cinnamon Swirl: In a small bowl, mix together brown sugar and ground cinnamon.
6. Prepare the Streusel Topping: In another bowl, combine brown sugar, flour, ground cinnamon, and melted vegan butter. Mix until crumbly.
7. Assemble the Coffee Cake: Pour half of the cake batter into the prepared baking pan.
8. Sprinkle the cinnamon swirl mixture evenly over the batter.
9. Pour the remaining batter over the cinnamon swirl.
10. Sprinkle the streusel topping over the top.
11. Bake in the preheated oven for 30-35 minutes or until a toothpick inserted into the center comes out clean.
12. Prepare the Glaze:
13. In a small bowl, whisk together powdered sugar, plant-based milk, and vanilla extract until smooth.
14. Once the coffee cake is cooled, drizzle the glaze over the top.

Gluten-Free Option:

- Substitute all-purpose flour with a gluten-free 1:1 flour blend.
- Add 1/2 teaspoon xanthan gum to the dry ingredients if the 1:1 flour doesn't have xanthan gum included.
- Ensure that the baking powder and baking soda are also gluten-free.

Raspberry Coffee Cake

Yield: 12 servings

Ingredients:

- For the Cake:
- 2 cups (250g) all-purpose flour
- 1 cup (200g) granulated sugar
- 1/2 cup (120ml) vegetable oil
- 1 cup (240ml) plant-based milk (such as almond or soy)
- 1 tablespoon (15ml) apple cider vinegar
- 1 teaspoon (5g) baking powder
- 1/2 teaspoon (3g) baking soda
- 1/4 teaspoon (1g) salt
- For the Raspberry Filling:
- 1 1/2 cups (225g) fresh raspberries
- 2 tablespoons (30g) granulated sugar
- 1 tablespoon (15ml) water
- 1 tablespoon (8g) cornstarch mixed with 2 tablespoons (30ml) water (for thickening)
- For the Streusel Topping:
- 1/2 cup (100g) brown sugar, packed
- 1/2 cup (60g) all-purpose flour
- 2 teaspoons (5g) ground cinnamon
- 1/4 cup (60g) vegan butter, melted
- For the Glaze:
- 1 cup (120g) powdered sugar
- 2 tablespoons (30ml) plant-based milk
- 1/2 teaspoon (3ml) vanilla extract

Directions:

1. Preheat your oven to 350°F (175°C). Grease a 9x13-inch baking pan.
2. Prepare the Cake:
3. In a large bowl, whisk together flour, sugar, baking powder, baking soda, and salt.
4. In a separate bowl, mix together vegetable oil, plant-based milk, and apple cider vinegar.
5. Pour the wet ingredients into the dry ingredients and stir until just combined. Avoid overmixing.
6. Prepare the Raspberry Filling:
7. In a saucepan over medium heat, combine fresh raspberries, sugar, and water.
8. Cook, stirring occasionally, until the raspberries break down and the mixture thickens, about 5-7 minutes.
9. Stir in the cornstarch-water mixture and cook for an additional 2 minutes until the filling thickens. Remove from heat and let it cool.
10. Prepare the Streusel Topping:
11. In a bowl, combine brown sugar, flour, ground cinnamon, and melted vegan butter. Mix until crumbly.
12. Assemble the Coffee Cake:
13. Pour half of the cake batter into the prepared baking pan.
14. Spoon the raspberry filling over the batter.
15. Pour the remaining batter over the raspberry filling.
16. Sprinkle the streusel topping over the top.
17. Bake in the preheated oven for 30-35 minutes or until a toothpick inserted into the center comes out clean.
18. Prepare the Glaze:
19. In a small bowl, whisk together powdered sugar, plant-based milk, and vanilla extract until smooth.
20. Once the coffee cake is cooled, drizzle the glaze over the top.

Lemon Pound Cake

Yield: 1 loaf

Ingredients:

- 1 1/2 cups (180g) all-purpose flour
- 1 teaspoon (5g) baking powder
- 1/2 teaspoon (3g) baking soda
- 1/4 teaspoon (2g) salt
- 1/2 cup (120g) vegan butter, softened
- 1 cup (200g) granulated sugar
- 2 tablespoons (30ml) lemon juice
- 1 tablespoon (15ml) lemon zest
- 1 teaspoon (5ml) vanilla extract
- 1 cup (240ml) plant-based milk (such as almond, soy, or oat)
- Lemon Glaze:
- 1 cup (120g) powdered sugar
- 2 tablespoons (30ml) fresh lemon juice
- 1 teaspoon (5ml) lemon zest

Directions:

1. Preheat your oven to 350°F (175°C). Grease and flour a loaf pan.
2. In a medium bowl, whisk together the flour, baking powder, baking soda, and salt.
3. In a large bowl, cream together the vegan butter and granulated sugar until light and fluffy.
4. Add the lemon juice, lemon zest, and vanilla extract to the butter-sugar mixture. Mix until well combined.
5. Gradually add the dry ingredients to the wet ingredients, alternating with the plant-based milk. Begin and end with the dry ingredients. Mix until just combined.
6. Pour the batter into the prepared loaf pan, spreading it evenly.
7. Bake for 45-55 minutes or until a toothpick inserted into the center comes out clean.
8. While the cake is baking, prepare the lemon glaze. In a small bowl, whisk together the powdered sugar, fresh lemon juice, and lemon zest until smooth.
9. Once the cake is out of the oven, let it cool in the pan for 10 minutes, then transfer it to a wire rack.
10. While the cake is still warm, drizzle the lemon glaze over the top.
11. Allow the cake to cool completely before slicing and serving.

Gluten-Free Option:

- Substitute all-purpose flour with a gluten-free 1:1 flour blend.
- Add 1/2 teaspoon xanthan gum to the dry ingredients if the 1:1 flour doesn't have xanthan gum included.
- Ensure that the baking powder and baking soda are also gluten-free.

Flourless Chocolate Cake

Yield: 1 cake (8-inch round)

Ingredients:

- 1 cup (200g) semisweet or bittersweet chocolate chips
- 1/2 cup (120g) vegan butter
- 3/4 cup (150g) granulated sugar
- 1/4 teaspoon (2g) salt
- 1 teaspoon (5ml) vanilla extract
- 3 large flax eggs (3 tablespoons (27g) ground flaxseed + 9 tablespoons (135ml) water)
- 1/2 cup (60g) cocoa powder, sifted
- Powdered sugar for dusting (optional)
- Vegan whipped cream or ice cream for serving (optional)

Directions:

1. Preheat your oven to 375°F (190°C). Grease an 8-inch round cake pan and line the bottom with parchment paper.
2. In a heatproof bowl, melt the chocolate chips and vegan butter together. This can be done using a double boiler or by microwaving in 20-second intervals, stirring between each interval until smooth.
3. Stir in the granulated sugar, salt, and vanilla extract into the melted chocolate mixture.
4. Prepare the flax eggs by mixing ground flaxseed with water in a small bowl. Let it sit for 5-10 minutes until it thickens.
5. Add the flax eggs to the chocolate mixture and stir until well combined.
6. Sift the cocoa powder over the chocolate mixture and fold it in until no streaks remain.
7. Pour the batter into the prepared cake pan, spreading it evenly.
8. Bake for 22-25 minutes or until a toothpick inserted into the center comes out with moist crumbs (not wet batter).
9. Allow the cake to cool in the pan for 10 minutes, then transfer it to a wire rack to cool completely.
10. Once cooled, dust with powdered sugar if desired.
11. Serve slices of the flourless chocolate cake on their own or with a dollop of vegan whipped cream or a scoop of dairy-free ice cream.

Gluten-Free Option:

- This cake is naturally gluten-free as it doesn't contain any flour. Ensure that the chocolate chips and cocoa powder used are gluten-free if you have specific dietary restrictions.

Chocolate Lava Cake

Yield: 4 individual cakes

Ingredients:

- 1/2 cup (120g) vegan butter
- 1 cup (175g) dairy-free chocolate chips
- 1/2 cup (60g) powdered sugar
- 1/3 cup (40g) all-purpose flour
- 1/4 teaspoon (2g) salt
- 2 teaspoons (10ml) vanilla extract
- 3 flax eggs (3 tablespoons (27g) ground flaxseed + 9 tablespoons (135ml) water)
- Vegan vanilla ice cream for serving (optional)
- Fresh berries for garnish (optional)
- Powdered sugar for dusting (optional)

Directions:

1. Preheat your oven to 425°F (220°C). Grease four ramekins and place them on a baking sheet.
2. In a heatproof bowl, melt the vegan butter and chocolate chips together. This can be done using a double boiler or by microwaving in 20-second intervals, stirring between each interval until smooth.
3. In a separate bowl, whisk together the powdered sugar, all-purpose flour, and salt.
4. Add the dry ingredients to the melted chocolate mixture and stir until well combined.
5. In another bowl, prepare the flax eggs by mixing ground flaxseed with water. Let it sit for 5-10 minutes until it thickens.
6. Add the flax eggs and vanilla extract to the chocolate mixture, stirring until smooth.
7. Divide the batter equally among the prepared ramekins.
8. Bake for 12-14 minutes or until the edges are set but the center is still soft.
9. Allow the lava cakes to cool for 2-3 minutes before running a knife around the edges and inverting them onto serving plates.
10. Serve the chocolate lava cakes warm with a scoop of vegan vanilla ice cream, fresh berries, and a dusting of powdered sugar if desired.

Gluten-Free Option:

- Substitute all-purpose flour with a gluten-free 1:1 flour blend.
- Add 1/4 teaspoon xanthan gum to the dry ingredients if the 1:1 flour doesn't have xanthan gum included.

Pineapple Carrot Cake

Yield: 1 cake (9-inch round)

Ingredients:

- 2 cups (250g) all-purpose flour
- 1 1/2 teaspoons (7g) baking powder
- 1 teaspoon (5g) baking soda
- 1/2 teaspoon (3g) salt
- 1 1/2 teaspoons (3g) ground cinnamon
- 1/2 teaspoon (1g) ground nutmeg
- 1/2 cup (120ml) vegetable oil
- 1 cup (200g) granulated sugar
- 1/2 cup (100g) brown sugar, packed
- 1/2 cup (120ml) unsweetened applesauce
- 1/4 cup (60ml) plant-based milk (such as almond, soy, or oat)
- 1 teaspoon (5ml) vanilla extract
- 2 cups (200g) grated carrots (about 3 medium carrots)
- 1 cup (150g) crushed pineapple, drained
- 1/2 cup (60g) chopped walnuts or pecans (optional)
- 1/2 cup (75g) raisins (optional)
- Vegan Cream Cheese Frosting:
- 8 oz (225g) vegan cream cheese, softened
- 1/4 cup (60g) vegan butter, softened
- 3 cups (360g) powdered sugar
- 1 teaspoon (5ml) vanilla extract

Gluten-Free Option:

- Substitute all-purpose flour with a gluten-free 1:1 flour blend.
- Add 1/2 teaspoon xanthan gum to the dry ingredients if the 1:1 flour doesn't have xanthan gum included.
- Ensure that the baking powder and baking soda are also gluten-free.

Directions:

1. Preheat your oven to 350°F (175°C). Grease and flour a 9-inch round cake pan.
2. In a medium bowl, whisk together the flour, baking powder, baking soda, salt, cinnamon, and nutmeg.
3. In a large bowl, whisk together the vegetable oil, granulated sugar, brown sugar, applesauce, plant-based milk, and vanilla extract until well combined.
4. Gradually add the dry ingredients to the wet ingredients, mixing until just combined.
5. Fold in the grated carrots, crushed pineapple, and, if desired, add the chopped nuts and raisins.
6. Pour the batter into the prepared cake pan, spreading it evenly.
7. Bake for 30-35 minutes or until a toothpick inserted into the center comes out clean.
8. Allow the cake to cool in the pan for 10 minutes, then transfer it to a wire rack to cool completely.
9. Vegan Cream Cheese Frosting: In a medium bowl, beat together the vegan cream cheese and vegan butter until smooth.
10. Add the powdered sugar and vanilla extract, and beat until creamy and well combined.
11. Assembling: Once the cake is completely cooled, frost the top with the vegan cream cheese frosting.
12. Optionally, garnish with additional chopped nuts or grated carrots.

Cherry Almond Cupcakes

Yield: 12 cupcakes

Ingredients:

- Cupcake Ingredients:
- 1 1/2 cups (180g) all-purpose flour
- 1 1/2 teaspoons (7g) baking powder
- 1/2 teaspoon (3g) baking soda
- 1/4 teaspoon (2g) salt
- 1/2 cup (120ml) almond milk
- 1 teaspoon (5ml) almond extract
- 1/2 cup (120ml) vegetable oil
- 3/4 cup (150g) granulated sugar
- 1/2 cup (75g) chopped cherries (fresh or frozen)
- Almond Buttercream Frosting:
- 1 cup (225g) vegan butter, softened
- 3 cups (360g) powdered sugar
- 1 teaspoon (5ml) almond extract
- 2-3 tablespoons (30-45ml) almond milk
- Sliced almonds for garnish (optional)
- Whole cherries for topping (optional)

Gluten-Free Option:

- Substitute all-purpose flour with a gluten-free 1:1 flour blend.
- Add 1/2 teaspoon xanthan gum to the dry ingredients if the 1:1 flour doesn't have xanthan gum included.
- Ensure that the baking powder and baking soda are also gluten-free.

Directions:

1. Preheat your oven to 350°F (175°C) and line a cupcake tin with paper liners.
2. In a medium bowl, whisk together the flour, baking powder, baking soda, and salt.
3. In a separate bowl, mix together the almond milk, almond extract, vegetable oil, and granulated sugar until well combined.
4. Gradually add the dry ingredients to the wet ingredients, mixing until just combined.
5. Gently fold in the chopped cherries.
6. Spoon the batter into the cupcake liners, filling each about 2/3 full.
7. Bake for 18-22 minutes or until a toothpick inserted into the center comes out clean.
8. Allow the cupcakes to cool in the tin for 5 minutes, then transfer them to a wire rack to cool completely.
9. Almond Buttercream Frosting:
10. In a large bowl, beat the vegan butter until creamy.
11. Add the powdered sugar, almond extract, and almond milk. Beat until smooth and fluffy.
12. Assembling:
13. Once the cupcakes are completely cooled, frost them with the almond buttercream frosting.
14. Garnish with sliced almonds and a whole cherry on top if desired.

Chocolate Beet Cake

Yield: 1 cake (9-inch round)

Ingredients:

- 2 cups (250g) all-purpose flour
- 1 1/2 teaspoons (7g) baking powder
- 1/2 teaspoon (3g) baking soda
- 1/4 teaspoon (2g) salt
- 1 cup (200g) granulated sugar
- 1/2 cup (50g) cocoa powder
- 1/2 cup (120ml) vegetable oil
- 1 cup (250g) cooked and pureed beets
- 1 cup (240ml) plant-based milk (such as almond, soy, or oat)
- 1 teaspoon (5ml) vanilla extract
- Chocolate Ganache:
- 1/2 cup (120ml) plant-based milk
- 1 cup (175g) dairy-free chocolate chips

Directions:

1. Preheat your oven to 350°F (175°C). Grease and flour a 9-inch round cake pan.
2. In a medium bowl, whisk together the flour, baking powder, baking soda, salt, and cocoa powder.
3. In a large bowl, whisk together the granulated sugar, vegetable oil, beet puree, plant-based milk, and vanilla extract until well combined.
4. Gradually add the dry ingredients to the wet ingredients, mixing until just combined.
5. Pour the batter into the prepared cake pan, spreading it evenly.
6. Bake for 30-35 minutes or until a toothpick inserted into the center comes out clean.
7. Allow the cake to cool in the pan for 10 minutes, then transfer it to a wire rack to cool completely.
8. Chocolate Ganache:
9. In a saucepan, heat the plant-based milk over medium heat until it starts to simmer.
10. Remove from heat and add the dairy-free chocolate chips. Let it sit for a minute, then whisk until smooth.
11. Let the ganache cool for a few minutes before pouring it over the cooled cake.

Gluten-Free Option:

- Substitute all-purpose flour with a gluten-free 1:1 flour blend.
- Add 1/2 teaspoon xanthan gum to the dry ingredients if the 1:1 flour doesn't have xanthan gum included.
- Ensure that the baking powder and baking soda are also gluten-free.

Dark Chocolate Pear Cake

Yield: 1 cake (9-inch round)

Ingredients:

- 2 cups (250g) all-purpose flour
- 1 1/2 teaspoons (7g) baking powder
- 1/2 teaspoon (3g) baking soda
- 1/4 teaspoon (2g) salt
- 1/2 cup (50g) cocoa powder
- 1/2 cup (120ml) vegetable oil
- 1 cup (200g) granulated sugar
- 1 cup (240ml) plant-based milk (such as almond, soy, or oat)
- 1 teaspoon (5ml) vanilla extract
- 2 ripe pears, peeled, cored, and diced
- Chocolate Glaze:
- 1/2 cup (120ml) plant-based milk
- 1 cup (175g) dairy-free dark chocolate chips

Directions:

1. Preheat your oven to 350°F (175°C). Grease and flour a 9-inch round cake pan.
2. In a medium bowl, whisk together the flour, baking powder, baking soda, salt, and cocoa powder.
3. In a large bowl, whisk together the vegetable oil, granulated sugar, plant-based milk, and vanilla extract until well combined.
4. Gradually add the dry ingredients to the wet ingredients, mixing until just combined.
5. Gently fold in the diced pears.
6. Pour the batter into the prepared cake pan, spreading it evenly.
7. Bake for 30-35 minutes or until a toothpick inserted into the center comes out clean.
8. Allow the cake to cool in the pan for 10 minutes, then transfer it to a wire rack to cool completely.
9. Chocolate Glaze:
10. In a saucepan, heat the plant-based milk over medium heat until it starts to simmer.
11. Remove from heat and add the dairy-free dark chocolate chips. Let it sit for a minute, then whisk until smooth.
12. Let the glaze cool for a few minutes before pouring it over the cooled cake.

Gluten-Free Option:

- Substitute all-purpose flour with a gluten-free 1:1 flour blend.
- Add 1/2 teaspoon xanthan gum to the dry ingredients if the 1:1 flour doesn't have xanthan gum included.
- Ensure that the baking powder and baking soda are also gluten-free.

Chocolate Vermouth Cake

Yield: 1 cake (9-inch round)

Ingredients:

- 2 cups (250g) all-purpose flour
- 1 1/2 teaspoons (7g) baking powder
- 1/2 teaspoon (3g) baking soda
- 1/4 teaspoon (2g) salt
- 1/2 cup (50g) cocoa powder
- 1/2 cup (120ml) vegetable oil
- 1 cup (200g) granulated sugar
- 1 cup (240ml) plant-based milk (such as almond, soy, or oat)
- 1/4 cup (60ml) sweet vermouth
- 1 teaspoon (5ml) vanilla extract
- Chocolate Vermouth Ganache:
- 1/2 cup (120ml) plant-based milk
- 1 cup (175g) dairy-free dark chocolate chips
- 2 tablespoons (30ml) sweet vermouth

Directions:

1. Preheat your oven to 350°F (175°C). Grease and flour a 9-inch round cake pan.
2. In a medium bowl, whisk together the flour, baking powder, baking soda, salt, and cocoa powder.
3. In a large bowl, whisk together the vegetable oil, granulated sugar, plant-based milk, sweet vermouth, and vanilla extract until well combined.
4. Gradually add the dry ingredients to the wet ingredients, mixing until just combined.
5. Pour the batter into the prepared cake pan, spreading it evenly.
6. Bake for 30-35 minutes or until a toothpick inserted into the center comes out clean.
7. Allow the cake to cool in the pan for 10 minutes, then transfer it to a wire rack to cool completely.
8. Chocolate Vermouth Ganache:
9. In a saucepan, heat the plant-based milk over medium heat until it starts to simmer.
10. Remove from heat and add the dairy-free dark chocolate chips and sweet vermouth. Let it sit for a minute, then whisk until smooth.
11. Let the ganache cool for a few minutes before pouring it over the cooled cake.

Gluten-Free Option:

- Substitute all-purpose flour with a gluten-free 1:1 flour blend.
- Add 1/2 teaspoon xanthan gum to the dry ingredients if the 1:1 flour doesn't have xanthan gum included.
- Ensure that the baking powder and baking soda are also gluten-free.

CHAPTER 6

Pies, Tarts, & Pastries

Vegan Pie Crust

Yield: 1 double-crust or 2 single-crust pies

Ingredients:

- 2 1/2 cups (300g) all-purpose flour
- 1 cup (226g) vegan butter, cold and cut into small cubes
- 1 tablespoon (12g) granulated sugar
- 1/2 teaspoon (3g) salt
- 6-8 tablespoons (90-120ml) ice-cold water

Directions:

1. In a large mixing bowl, combine the all-purpose flour, granulated sugar, and salt.
2. Add the cold, cubed vegan butter to the flour mixture.
3. Using a pastry cutter or your hands, work the butter into the flour until the mixture resembles coarse crumbs. You should still see small, pea-sized pieces of butter.
4. Gradually add the ice-cold water, one tablespoon at a time, mixing with a fork or your hands after each addition. Continue adding water until the dough comes together and can be formed into a ball.
5. Divide the dough in half if making a double-crust pie or leave it as a whole for a single-crust pie. Shape each portion into a disk, wrap in plastic wrap, and refrigerate for at least 1 hour or overnight.
6. Preheat your oven according to your pie recipe instructions.
7. Roll out the chilled dough on a floured surface to fit your pie dish. Place the rolled-out dough into the pie dish and trim any excess.
8. Fill the pie crust with your desired filling and follow the baking instructions for your specific pie recipe.

Gluten-Free Option:

- Substitute all-purpose flour with a gluten-free 1:1 flour blend.
- Ensure that the vegan butter used is labeled gluten-free.
- Add 1/2 teaspoon xanthan gum to the flour mixture if the gluten-free flour blend doesn't include it.

Vegan Tart Crust

Yield: 1 10" tart crust

Ingredients:

- 1 1/2 cups (180g) all-purpose flour
- 1/2 cup (113g) vegan butter, cold and cut into small cubes
- 2 tablespoons (25g) granulated sugar
- 1/4 teaspoon (2g) salt
- 2-3 tablespoons (30-45ml) ice-cold water

Directions:

1. In a food processor, combine the all-purpose flour, granulated sugar, and salt. Pulse a few times to mix.
2. Add the cold, cubed vegan butter to the food processor.
3. Pulse the mixture until it resembles coarse crumbs. You should still see small, pea-sized pieces of butter.
4. Gradually add the ice-cold water, one tablespoon at a time, pulsing after each addition. Continue adding water until the dough starts to come together.
5. Transfer the dough to a floured surface and shape it into a disk. Wrap it in plastic wrap and refrigerate for at least 30 minutes.
6. Preheat your oven according to your tart recipe instructions.
7. Roll out the chilled dough on a floured surface to fit your tart pan. Press the dough into the pan, ensuring an even thickness on the bottom and up the sides.
8. Trim any excess dough and prick the bottom of the crust with a fork.
9. Follow the baking instructions for your specific tart recipe.

Gluten-Free Option:

- Substitute all-purpose flour with a gluten-free 1:1 flour blend.
- Ensure that the vegan butter used is labeled gluten-free.
- Add 1/2 teaspoon xanthan gum to the flour mixture if the gluten-free flour blend doesn't include it.

Chocolate Ganache Tart

Yield: 1 tart

Ingredients:

- 1 Vegan Tart Crust (Refer to the "Vegan Tart Crust" recipe at the beginning of this chapter.)
- 1 cup (240ml) plant-based milk
- 2 cups (350g) dairy-free dark chocolate chips
- 2 tablespoons (30ml) maple syrup
- 1/4 teaspoon (2g) salt
- For Garnish
- Fresh berries (optional)
- Toasted hazelnuts chopped (optional)
- Vegan whipped cream (optional)

Directions:

1. Prepare the Vegan Tart Crust:
2. Follow the instructions for the "Vegan Tart Crust" recipe at the beginning of this chapter or use a store-bought vegan pie crust. Pre-bake the crust according to the tart recipe instructions.
3. Make the Chocolate Ganache:
4. In a saucepan, heat the plant-based milk until it starts to simmer.
5. Remove from heat and add the dairy-free dark chocolate chips, maple syrup, and salt.
6. Let it sit for a minute, then whisk until smooth.
7. Assemble the Tart:
8. Pour the chocolate ganache into the pre-baked tart crust, spreading it evenly.
9. Refrigerate the tart for at least 2 hours or until the ganache is set.
10. Garnish and Serve:
11. Garnish the tart with fresh berries, toasted hazelnuts, or vegan whipped cream if desired.
12. Slice and serve chilled. Enjoy your decadent vegan chocolate ganache tart!

Gluten-Free Option:

- Substitute the tart crust with a gluten-free version using the "Vegan Tart Crust" recipe modifications.

Classic Pumpkin Pie

Yield: 1 pie

Ingredients:

- 1 Vegan Pie Crust (Refer to the "Vegan Pie Crust" recipe at the beginning of this chapter or use a store-bought vegan pie crust.)
- 1 can (15 oz) (425g) pumpkin puree
- 3/4 cup (150g) granulated sugar
- 1/2 cup (120ml) canned coconut milk (full-fat)
- 1/4 cup (60ml) maple syrup
- 1 tablespoon (7g) cornstarch
- 1 teaspoon (3g) ground cinnamon
- 1/2 teaspoon (2g) ground ginger
- 1/4 teaspoon (1g) ground nutmeg
- 1/4 teaspoon (1g) salt
- 1/8 teaspoon ground cloves
- Vegan whipped cream for serving (optional)

Directions:

1. Prepare the Vegan Pie Crust:
2. Follow the instructions for the "Vegan Pie Crust" recipe at the beginning of this chapter or use a store-bought vegan pie crust. Pre-bake the crust according to the pie recipe instructions.
3. Make the Pumpkin Filling:
4. In a large bowl, whisk together the pumpkin puree, granulated sugar, coconut milk, maple syrup, cornstarch, ground cinnamon, ground ginger, ground nutmeg, salt, and ground cloves until well combined.
5. Assemble and Bake:
6. Preheat your oven to 425°F (220°C).
7. Pour the pumpkin filling into the pre-baked pie crust, spreading it evenly.
8. Bake in the preheated oven for 15 minutes, then reduce the oven temperature to 350°F (175°C) and continue baking for an additional 40-50 minutes or until the center is set.
9. Allow the pie to cool completely before refrigerating for at least 4 hours or overnight to set.
10. Serve:
11. Slice the chilled pumpkin pie and serve with a dollop of vegan whipped cream if desired.

Gluten-Free Option:

- Substitute the pie crust with a gluten-free version using the "Vegan Pie Crust" recipe modifications or Ensure the store-bought pie crust is gluten-free.

Fruit Tart with Vanilla Cashew Cream

Yield: 1 tart

Ingredients:

- 1 Vegan Tart Crust (Refer to the "Vegan Tart Crust" recipe at the beginning of this chapter.)
- 1 cup (150g) raw cashews, soaked in hot water for 1-2 hours
- 1/3 cup (80ml) coconut milk
- 1/4 cup (60ml) maple syrup
- 2 teaspoons (10ml) vanilla extract
- Pinch of salt
- Assorted fresh fruits (berries, kiwi, grapes, etc.) for topping

Directions:

1. Prepare the Vegan Tart Crust:
2. Follow the instructions for the "Vegan Tart Crust" recipe at the beginning of this chapter or use a store-bought vegan pie crust. Pre-bake the crust according to the tart recipe instructions.
3. Make the Vanilla Cashew Cream:
4. In a blender, combine the soaked cashews (drained), coconut milk, maple syrup, vanilla extract, and a pinch of salt.
5. Blend until smooth and creamy, scraping down the sides as needed. Adjust sweetness to taste.
6. Assemble the Fruit Tart:
7. Once the tart crust has cooled, spread the vanilla cashew cream evenly over the crust.
8. Arrange Fresh Fruits:
9. Arrange assorted fresh fruits on top of the cashew cream. Get creative with the arrangement to make the tart visually appealing.
10. Chill and Serve:
11. Refrigerate the fruit tart for at least 1-2 hours to allow the cashew cream to set before slicing.

Gluten-Free Option:

- Substitute the tart crust with a gluten-free version using the "Vegan Tart Crust" recipe modifications.

Key Lime Pie

Yield: 1 pie

Ingredients:

- 1 Vegan Pie Crust (Refer to the "Vegan Pie Crust" recipe at the beginning of this chapter or use a store-bought vegan pie crust.)
- 1 1/2 cups (375ml) key lime juice (about 20-25 key limes)
- 2 cans (28 oz total) (800g) coconut cream, chilled
- 1 cup (200g) granulated sugar
- 1/2 cup (120ml) melted coconut oil
- 1 tablespoon (7g) cornstarch
- Zest of 2 key limes (optional, for garnish)
- Vegan whipped cream for serving (optional)

Gluten-Free Option:

- Substitute the pie crust with a gluten-free version using the "Vegan Pie Crust" recipe modifications. Ensure the store-bought pie crust is gluten-free if using.

Directions:

1. Prepare the Vegan Pie Crust:
2. Follow the instructions for the "Vegan Pie Crust" recipe at the beginning of this chapter or use a store-bought vegan pie crust. Pre-bake the crust according to the pie recipe instructions.
3. Make the Key Lime Filling:
4. In a large bowl, whisk together the key lime juice, coconut cream, granulated sugar, melted coconut oil, and cornstarch until well combined and smooth.
5. Assemble and Chill:
6. Pour the key lime filling into the pre-baked pie crust, spreading it evenly.
7. Refrigerate:
8. Refrigerate the key lime pie for at least 4 hours or overnight to allow it to set.
9. Garnish and Serve:
10. Before serving, garnish with key lime zest and a dollop of vegan whipped cream if desired.

Apple Fritters

Yield: Approximately 12 fritters

Ingredients:

- 2 cups (250g) all-purpose flour
- 1/4 cup (50g) granulated sugar
- 1 tablespoon (15g) baking powder
- 1/2 teaspoon (3g) salt
- 1 teaspoon (5g) ground cinnamon
- 1/2 teaspoon (1g) ground nutmeg
- 3/4 cup (180ml) plant-based milk (such as almond, soy, or oat)
- 1 teaspoon (5ml) vanilla extract
- 2 cups (about 2 medium-sized) apples, peeled and diced into small pieces
- Vegetable oil for frying
- Powdered sugar for dusting

Directions:

1. Prepare the Batter:
2. In a large bowl, whisk together the all-purpose flour, granulated sugar, baking powder, salt, ground cinnamon, and ground nutmeg.
3. Add Wet Ingredients:
4. Pour in the plant-based milk and vanilla extract. Stir until just combined. The batter should have a thick consistency.
5. Fold in Apples:
6. Gently fold in the diced apples until they are evenly distributed throughout the batter.
7. Heat Oil:
8. In a deep skillet or pot, heat vegetable oil to 350°F (180°C).
9. Fry the Fritters:
10. Using a spoon or cookie scoop, carefully drop portions of the batter into the hot oil. Fry until the fritters are golden brown on both sides, turning them as needed. This should take about 2-3 minutes per side.
11. Drain and Cool:
12. Remove the fritters from the oil and place them on a plate lined with paper towels to drain excess oil.
13. Garnish
14. Once the fritters have cooled slightly, dust them with powdered sugar.

Gluten-Free Option:

- Substitute all-purpose flour with a gluten-free 1:1 flour blend.
- Add 1/2 teaspoon xanthan gum to the dry ingredients if the gluten-free flour blend doesn't include it.
- Ensure the baking powder is also gluten-free.

Banana Rum Tart

Yield: 1 tart

Ingredients:

- 1 Vegan Tart Crust (Refer to the "Vegan Tart Crust" recipe at the beginning of this chapter.)
- 4 ripe bananas, sliced
- 1/2 cup (120ml) coconut cream
- 1/4 cup (60ml) dark rum
- 1/3 cup (80g) brown sugar
- 1 tablespoon (15g) cornstarch
- 1 teaspoon (5ml) vanilla extract
- Pinch of salt
- 1/4 cup (25g) shredded coconut (optional, for garnish)

Directions:

1. Prepare the Vegan Tart Crust:
2. Follow the instructions for the "Vegan Tart Crust" recipe at the beginning of this chapter. Pre-bake the crust according to the tart recipe instructions.
3. Make the Banana Rum Filling:
4. In a saucepan, combine coconut cream, dark rum, brown sugar, cornstarch, vanilla extract, and a pinch of salt. Whisk until smooth.
5. Place the saucepan over medium heat and bring the mixture to a gentle boil, stirring constantly. Once it thickens, remove it from heat.
6. Assemble the Tart:
7. Arrange the sliced bananas on the pre-baked tart crust.
8. Pour the warm banana rum filling over the sliced bananas, ensuring an even distribution.
9. Optional: Garnish with Coconut:
10. Sprinkle shredded coconut on top for an optional garnish.
11. Chill and Serve:
12. Refrigerate the banana rum tart for at least 2 hours or until the filling is set.

Gluten-Free Option:

- Substitute the tart crust with a gluten-free version using the "Vegan Tart Crust" recipe modifications.

Mango Coconut Cream Tart

Yield: 1 tart

Ingredients:

- 1 Vegan Tart Crust (Refer to the "Vegan Tart Crust" recipe at the beginning of this chapter or use a store-bought vegan pie crust.)
- 2 large ripe mangoes, peeled and diced
- 1 can (13.5 oz) (400ml) coconut milk, chilled
- 1/3 cup (80g) granulated sugar
- 1/4 cup (30g) cornstarch
- 1 teaspoon (5ml) vanilla extract
- Zest of 1 lime
- 1/4 cup (25g) shredded coconut, toasted (optional, for garnish)

Gluten-Free Option:

- Substitute the tart crust with a gluten-free version using the "Vegan Tart Crust" recipe modifications. Ensure the store-bought pie crust is gluten-free if using.

Directions:

1. Prepare the Vegan Tart Crust:
2. Follow the instructions for the "Vegan Tart Crust" recipe at the beginning of this chapter. Pre-bake the crust according to the tart recipe instructions.
3. Make the Mango Coconut Cream Filling:
4. In a blender, puree the diced mangoes until smooth.
5. Open the chilled can of coconut milk without shaking it. Scoop out the thick coconut cream that has separated at the top and place it in a bowl.
6. In a saucepan, combine the coconut cream, granulated sugar, cornstarch, and vanilla extract. Whisk over medium heat until the mixture thickens.
7. Allow the coconut cream mixture to cool slightly, then fold in the mango puree and lime zest until well combined.
8. Assemble the Tart:
9. Pour the mango coconut cream filling into the pre-baked tart crust.
10. Toast shredded coconut in a dry pan over medium heat until golden brown. Sprinkle the toasted coconut over the tart for an optional garnish.
11. Refrigerate the mango coconut cream tart for at least 2 hours or until the filling is set.

Coconut Panna Cotta

Yield: 4 servings

Ingredients:

- 1 can (13.5 oz) (400ml) full-fat coconut milk
- 1/4 cup (60g) granulated sugar
- 1 teaspoon (5ml) vanilla extract
- 2 teaspoons (4g) agar-agar powder
- 2 tablespoons (30ml) water
- Fresh berries or fruit for topping
- Mint leaves for garnish (optional)

Directions:

1. Prepare Panna Cotta Base:
2. In a saucepan, combine the coconut milk, granulated sugar, and vanilla extract. Heat over medium heat, stirring occasionally, until the mixture is warm and the sugar has dissolved. Do not bring it to a boil.
3. In a small bowl, mix the agar-agar powder with water. Let it sit for a few minutes to activate.
4. Add the activated agar-agar mixture to the coconut milk mixture. Stir well to combine.
5. Bring the mixture to a gentle simmer over medium heat. Continue simmering for 5-7 minutes, stirring constantly, until the agar-agar is fully dissolved.
6. Pour into Molds & Chill:
7. Remove the saucepan from heat. Pour the coconut mixture into individual molds or serving glasses.
8. Allow the panna cotta to cool to room temperature before placing it in the refrigerator to set. Refrigerate for at least 4 hours or until fully set.
9. Serve:
10. Once set, remove the coconut panna cotta from the molds or serve directly in glasses.
11. Top with fresh berries or fruit of your choice. Garnish with mint leaves if desired.

Gluten-Free Option:

- Ensure all ingredients are gluten-free, as agar-agar is naturally gluten-free.

Herbed Tomato Balsamic Tart

Yield: 1 tart

Ingredients:

- 1 Vegan Tart Crust (Refer to the "Vegan Tart Crust" recipe at the beginning of this chapter or use a store-bought vegan pie crust.)
- 4 large tomatoes, thinly sliced
- 1/4 cup (60ml) balsamic vinegar
- 2 tablespoons (30ml) olive oil
- 2 cloves garlic, minced
- 1 teaspoon (3g) dried oregano
- 1 teaspoon (3g) dried basil
- Salt and black pepper to taste
- Fresh basil leaves for garnish

Directions:

1. Prepare the Vegan Tart Crust:
2. Follow the instructions for the "Vegan Tart Crust" recipe at the beginning of this chapter. Pre-bake the crust according to the tart recipe instructions.
3. Preheat Oven:
4. Preheat the oven to 375°F (190°C).
5. Prepare Tart filling:
6. Place the thinly sliced tomatoes on paper towels to absorb excess moisture.
7. Arrange the tomato slices on the pre-baked tart crust, slightly overlapping them.
8. In a small bowl, whisk together balsamic vinegar, olive oil, minced garlic, dried oregano, dried basil, salt, and black pepper.
9. Drizzle the balsamic herb marinade over the arranged tomatoes.
10. Bake & Serve:
11. Bake the tart in the preheated oven for about 20-25 minutes or until the crust is golden and the tomatoes are tender.
12. Allow the tart to cool for a few minutes before garnishing.
13. Garnish the tart with fresh basil leaves just before serving.

Gluten-Free Option:

- Substitute the tart crust with a gluten-free version using the "Vegan Tart Crust" recipe modifications.

Ginger Fig Tart with Coconut Crust

Yield: 1 tart

Ingredients:

- Coconut Tart Crust Ingredients:
- 1 cup (120g) almond flour
- 1 cup (80g) shredded coconut, unsweetened
- 1/4 cup (60ml) coconut oil, melted
- 2 tablespoons (30ml) maple syrup
- 1/2 teaspoon vanilla extract
- Pinch of salt
- Ginger Fig Filling Ingredients:
- 1 cup (about 10-12) dried figs, stems removed and halved
- 1/4 cup (60ml) maple syrup
- 1 tablespoon (15g) fresh ginger, grated
- 1 teaspoon (5ml) vanilla extract
- 1/4 cup (30g) cornstarch
- 1/4 teaspoon ground cinnamon
- Pinch of salt
- Optional Garnish:
- 1/4 cup (25g) shredded coconut, toasted

Directions:

1. Prepare the Coconut Tart Crust:
2. Preheat the oven to 350°F (175°C).
3. In a food processor, combine almond flour, shredded coconut, melted coconut oil, maple syrup, vanilla extract, and a pinch of salt.
4. Pulse until the mixture comes together and forms a dough-like consistency.
5. Press the crust mixture into the bottom and up the sides of a tart pan.
6. Bake in a preheated oven for 10-12 minutes or until the crust is golden brown. Allow it to cool.
7. Soak Dried Figs:
8. Place the dried figs in a bowl and cover them with hot water. Let them soak for about 15-20 minutes until they soften.
9. Make Ginger Fig Filling:
10. In a food processor, combine the soaked figs (drained), maple syrup, grated fresh ginger, vanilla extract, cornstarch, ground cinnamon, and a pinch of salt. Blend until smooth.
11. Pour the ginger fig filling into the pre-baked coconut tart crust, spreading it evenly.
12. Bake:
13. Bake the tart in the preheated oven for about 20-25 minutes or until the filling is set.
14. Allow the ginger fig tart to cool completely.
15. If desired, sprinkle toasted shredded coconut over the top of the tart for an additional layer of flavor and texture.

Cornflake Tart

Yield: 1 tart

Ingredients:

- Shortcrust Pastry:
- 1 1/2 cups (180g) all-purpose flour
- 1/2 cup (120g) vegan butter, cold and cubed
- 1/4 cup (50g) granulated sugar
- 2-3 tablespoons (30-45ml) ice-cold water
- Filling:
- 1/2 cup (120g) vegan butter
- 1/3 cup (80g) golden syrup or maple syrup
- 1/2 cup (120g) smooth peanut butter
- 4 cups (100g) cornflakes

Directions:

1. Prepare Shortcrust Pastry:
2. In a food processor, combine all-purpose flour, cold cubed vegan butter, and granulated sugar.
3. Pulse until the mixture resembles breadcrumbs.
4. Add ice-cold water, one tablespoon at a time, pulsing until the dough comes together.
5. Shape the dough into a disk, wrap it in plastic wrap, and refrigerate for 30 minutes.
6. Preheat the oven to 350°F (175°C).
7. Roll Out Pastry:
8. On a floured surface, roll out the chilled pastry to fit your tart pan.
9. Press the rolled-out pastry into a tart pan, trimming any excess. Prick the base with a fork.
10. Blind Bake:
11. Line the pastry with parchment paper and fill with baking beans or rice.
12. Blind bake the pastry in the preheated oven for 15 minutes. Remove the beans and parchment paper, then bake for an additional 5 minutes until lightly golden.
13. Prepare Filling:
14. In a saucepan, melt vegan butter, golden syrup (or maple syrup), and peanut butter over low heat. Stir until well combined.
15. Gently fold in the cornflakes until they are evenly coated with the peanut butter mixture.
16. Pour the cornflake mixture into the pre-baked tart shell, spreading it evenly.
17. Bake:
18. Bake the cornflake tart in the oven for 10-15 minutes until the filling is set.
19. Allow the cornflake tart to cool before slicing. Serve it at room temperature.

Gluten-Free Option:

- Substitute all-purpose flour with a gluten-free 1:1 flour blend for the shortcrust pastry.
- Ensure that the cornflakes used are gluten-free.

Apple Frangipane Tart

Yield: 1 tart

Ingredients:

- Shortcrust Pastry:
- 1 1/2 cups (180g) all-purpose flour
- 1/2 cup (120g) vegan butter, cold and cubed
- 1/4 cup (50g) granulated sugar
- 2-3 tablespoons (30-45ml) ice-cold water
- Frangipane Filling:
- 1 cup (100g) almond flour
- 1/4 cup (30g) all-purpose flour
- 1/2 cup (100g) granulated sugar
- 1/4 cup (60ml) almond milk
- 1/4 cup (60g) vegan butter, melted
- 1 teaspoon (5ml) vanilla extract
- Apple Topping:
- 2-3 apples, peeled, cored, and thinly sliced
- 1 tablespoon (15ml) lemon juice
- 2 tablespoons (30g) apricot jam (for glazing)

Directions:

1. Prepare Shortcrust Pastry:
2. In a food processor, combine all-purpose flour, cold cubed vegan butter, and granulated sugar.
3. Pulse until the mixture resembles breadcrumbs.
4. Add ice-cold water, one tablespoon at a time, pulsing until the dough comes together.
5. Shape the dough into a disk, wrap it in plastic wrap, and refrigerate for 30 minutes.
6. Preheat the oven to 350°F (175°C).
7. Roll Out Pastry:
8. On a floured surface, roll out the chilled pastry to fit your tart pan.
9. Press the rolled-out pastry into a tart pan, trimming any excess. Prick the base with a fork.
10. Blind Bake:
11. Line the pastry with parchment paper and fill with baking beans or rice.
12. Blind bake the pastry in the preheated oven for 15 minutes. Remove the beans and parchment paper, then bake for an additional 5 minutes until lightly golden.
13. Prepare Frangipane Filling:
14. In a bowl, whisk together almond flour, all-purpose flour, granulated sugar, almond milk, melted vegan butter, and vanilla extract until smooth.
15. Spread the frangipane filling evenly over the pre-baked tart shell.
16. Prepare Apple Topping:
17. Toss the thinly sliced apples with lemon juice to prevent browning.
18. Arrange the apple slices in a decorative pattern over the frangipane filling.
19. Bake:
20. Bake the tart in the oven for 25-30 minutes or until the frangipane is set and the apples are tender.
21. In a small saucepan, heat apricot jam until melted. Brush the melted jam over the arranged apple slices for a glossy finish.
22. Allow the tart to cool before slicing. Serve it at room temperature.

Gluten-Free Option:

- Substitute all-purpose flour with a gluten-free 1:1 flour blend plus an additional ½ teaspoon xanthan gum.

Apple Cranberry Gingersnap Pie

Yield: 1 pie

Ingredients:

- Gingersnap Crust:
- 2 cups (about 200g) gingersnap cookies, crushed
- 1/2 cup (115g) vegan butter, melted
- Apple Cranberry Filling:
- 4 cups (about 4 medium-sized) apples, peeled, cored, and thinly sliced
- 1 1/2 cups (150g) fresh or frozen cranberries
- 1 cup (200g) granulated sugar
- 1 tablespoon (15ml) orange zest
- 1/4 cup (60ml) orange juice
- 2 tablespoons (16g) cornstarch
- 1 teaspoon ground cinnamon
- 1/4 teaspoon ground nutmeg
- Pecan Streusel Topping:
- 1/2 cup (60g) all-purpose flour
- 1/2 cup (50g) chopped pecans
- 1/4 cup (50g) brown sugar, packed
- 1/4 cup (60g) vegan butter, cold and cubed

Directions:

1. Prepare Gingersnap Crust:
2. Preheat the oven to 350°F (175°C).
3. In a food processor, crush gingersnap cookies until fine crumbs form.
4. Combine the gingersnap crumbs with melted vegan butter in a bowl.
5. Press the mixture into the bottom and up the sides of a pie dish to form the crust.
6. Prepare Apple Cranberry Filling:
7. In a large bowl, combine sliced apples, cranberries, granulated sugar, orange zest, orange juice, cornstarch, ground cinnamon, and ground nutmeg.
8. Toss until the fruit is evenly coated.
9. Pour the apple cranberry filling into the prepared gingersnap crust.
10. Prepare Pecan Streusel Topping:
11. In a bowl, combine all-purpose flour, chopped pecans, brown sugar, and cold cubed vegan butter.
12. Using your fingers or a pastry cutter, mix until crumbly.
13. Sprinkle the pecan streusel topping over the apple cranberry filling.
14. Bake:
15. Bake the pie in the preheated oven for 35-40 minutes or until the streusel is golden brown, and the fruit is bubbly.
16. Allow the apple cranberry gingersnap pie to cool before slicing. Serve it at room temperature.

Gluten-Free Option:

- Substitute gingersnap cookies with gluten-free gingersnap cookies for the crust.
- Ensure that the all-purpose flour used in the streusel topping is gluten-free.

Eggnog Custard Tart

Yield: 1 tart

Ingredients:

- 1 vegan tart crust (from recipe at the beginning of this chapter)
- 2 cups (480ml) plant-based eggnog
- 1/2 cup (100g) granulated sugar
- 1/4 cup (30g) cornstarch
- 1 teaspoon (5ml) vanilla extract
- 1/2 teaspoon ground nutmeg
- 1/4 teaspoon ground cinnamon
- Pinch of salt

Directions:

1. Preheat the oven to 350°F (175°C).
2. Prepare tart crust from the recipe at the beginning of this chapter.
3. In a saucepan, whisk together plant-based eggnog, granulated sugar, cornstarch, vanilla extract, ground nutmeg, ground cinnamon, and a pinch of salt.
4. Cook over medium heat, stirring constantly, until the mixture thickens. Remove from heat.
5. Pour the eggnog custard filling into the pre-baked tart shell.
6. Bake the tart in the preheated oven for 20-25 minutes or until the custard is set.
7. Allow the eggnog custard tart to cool before slicing. Serve it at room temperature.

Gluten-Free Option:

- Substitute the tart crust with a gluten-free version using the "Vegan Tart Crust" recipe modifications.

Bourbon Peach Cobbler

Yield: 8 servings

Ingredients:

- Peach Filling:
- 6 cups (about 6-8 peaches) fresh or frozen peaches, peeled and sliced
- 1/2 cup (100g) granulated sugar
- 2 tablespoons (16g) cornstarch
- 1 tablespoon (15ml) lemon juice
- 2 tablespoons (30ml) bourbon
- Cobbler Topping:
- 1 cup (120g) all-purpose flour
- 1/2 cup (100g) granulated sugar
- 1 teaspoon (5g) baking powder
- 1/2 teaspoon (3g) baking soda
- 1/4 teaspoon (2g) salt
- 1/2 cup (120ml) plant-based milk (such as almond, soy, or oat)
- 1/4 cup (60ml) vegetable oil
- 1 teaspoon (5ml) vanilla extract

Directions:

1. Preheat the oven to 375°F (190°C).
2. In a large mixing bowl, combine sliced peaches, granulated sugar, cornstarch, lemon juice, and bourbon. Toss until the peaches are evenly coated.
3. Transfer the peach mixture to a greased 9x13-inch baking dish.
4. In a separate bowl, whisk together all-purpose flour, granulated sugar, baking powder, baking soda, and salt.
5. Add plant-based milk, vegetable oil, and vanilla extract to the dry ingredients. Stir until just combined.
6. Drop spoonfuls of the cobbler batter over the peach mixture.
7. Bake in the preheated oven for 35-40 minutes or until the cobbler topping is golden brown and cooked through.
8. Allow the bourbon peach cobbler to cool for a few minutes before serving.
9. Serve the cobbler warm, optionally topped with vegan vanilla ice cream or whipped cream.

Gluten-Free Option:

- Substitute all-purpose flour with a gluten-free 1:1 flour blend for the cobbler topping.

Mixed Berry Cobbler

Yield: 8 servings

Ingredients:

- Berry Filling:
- 4 cups mixed berries (strawberries, blueberries, raspberries, blackberries)
- 1/2 cup (100g) granulated sugar
- 2 tablespoons (16g) cornstarch
- 1 tablespoon (15ml) lemon juice
- Zest of one lemon
- Cobbler Topping:
- 1 cup (120g) all-purpose flour
- 1/2 cup (100g) granulated sugar
- 1 teaspoon (5g) baking powder
- 1/2 teaspoon (3g) baking soda
- 1/4 teaspoon (2g) salt
- 1/2 cup (120ml) plant-based milk (such as almond, soy, or oat)
- 1/4 cup (60ml) vegetable oil
- 1 teaspoon (5ml) vanilla extract

Directions:

1. Preheat the oven to 375°F (190°C).
2. In a large mixing bowl, combine mixed berries, granulated sugar, cornstarch, lemon juice, and lemon zest. Toss until the berries are evenly coated.
3. Transfer the mixed berry mixture to a greased 9x13-inch baking dish.
4. In a separate bowl, whisk together all-purpose flour, granulated sugar, baking powder, baking soda, and salt.
5. Add plant-based milk, vegetable oil, and vanilla extract to the dry ingredients. Stir until just combined.
6. Drop spoonfuls of the cobbler batter over the mixed berries.
7. Bake in the preheated oven for 35-40 minutes or until the cobbler topping is golden brown and cooked through.
8. Allow the mixed berry cobbler to cool for a few minutes before serving.
9. Serve the cobbler warm, optionally topped with vegan vanilla ice cream or whipped cream.

Gluten-Free Option:

- Substitute all-purpose flour with a gluten-free 1:1 flour blend for the cobbler topping.

Vegan Apple Strudel

Yield: 1 strudel

Ingredients:

- Filling:
- 4 large apples, peeled, cored, and thinly sliced
- 1/2 cup (100g) granulated sugar
- 1 teaspoon (3g) ground cinnamon
- 1/2 cup (60g) raisins
- 1/2 cup (50g) chopped walnuts or pecans
- Zest of one lemon
- 2 tablespoons (30ml) lemon juice
- Strudel Dough:
- 2 cups (250g) all-purpose flour
- 1/2 teaspoon (3g) salt
- 2 tablespoons (30ml) vegetable oil
- 3/4 cup (180ml) warm water
- Topping:
- 2 tablespoons (30g) vegan butter, melted
- 1 tablespoon (8g) granulated sugar
- Powdered sugar for dusting (optional)

Directions:

1. Prepare Filling:
2. Preheat the oven to 375°F (190°C).
3. In a large bowl, combine sliced apples, granulated sugar, ground cinnamon, raisins, chopped nuts, lemon zest, and lemon juice. Toss until well coated and set aside.
4. Prepare Strudel Dough:
5. In a large mixing bowl, combine all-purpose flour and salt. Make a well in the center and add vegetable oil and warm water.
6. Mix until a dough forms, then knead on a floured surface for a few minutes until smooth.
7. Roll Out Dough:
8. Roll out the strudel dough on a floured surface into a large rectangle, approximately 14x18 inches.
9. Add Filling:
10. Place the apple filling along one long edge of the dough, leaving a border around the edges.
11. Fold and Seal:
12. Fold the short edges of the dough over the filling, then roll the strudel tightly from the long edge. Place it seam-side down on a baking sheet.
13. Brush with Butter and Sugar:
14. Brush the top of the strudel with melted vegan butter and sprinkle with granulated sugar.
15. Bake:
16. Bake in the preheated oven for 30-35 minutes or until golden brown.
17. Allow the apple strudel to cool slightly before dusting with powdered sugar, if desired.
18. Serve slices of the apple strudel warm. It can be enjoyed on its own or with a scoop of vegan vanilla ice cream.

Gluten-Free Option:

- Substitute all-purpose flour with a gluten-free 1:1 flour blend for the strudel dough.

Blueberry Cream Cheese Danish

Yield: 8 pastries

Ingredients:

- Danish Dough:
- 2 1/4 teaspoons (7g) active dry yeast
- 1/4 cup (60ml) warm water
- 1/2 cup (120ml) plant-based milk (such as almond, soy, or oat)
- 1/4 cup (50g) granulated sugar
- 1/2 cup (113g) vegan butter, softened
- 2 1/2 cups (300g) all-purpose flour
- 1/2 teaspoon (3g) salt
- Cream Cheese Filling:
- 1 cup (240g) vegan cream cheese, softened
- 1/4 cup (50g) granulated sugar
- 1 teaspoon (5ml) vanilla extract
- Blueberry Filling:
- 1 cup (150g) fresh or frozen blueberries
- 2 tablespoons (30g) granulated sugar
- 1 tablespoon (8g) cornstarch
- 1 tablespoon (15ml) lemon juice
- Glaze:
- 1/2 cup (60g) powdered sugar
- 1-2 tablespoons (15-30ml) plant-based milk
- 1/2 teaspoon (2.5ml) vanilla extract

Gluten-Free Option:

- Substitute all-purpose flour with a gluten-free 1:1 flour blend for the Danish dough.

Directions:

1. Prepare Dough: In a small bowl, dissolve the active dry yeast in warm water. Let it sit for 5 minutes until it becomes frothy.
2. In a large mixing bowl, combine the activated yeast mixture, plant-based milk, granulated sugar, softened vegan butter, all-purpose flour, and salt. Mix until a dough forms.
3. Knead the dough on a floured surface for about 5 minutes, or until it becomes smooth. Place it in a greased bowl, cover, and let it rise in a warm place for 1-1.5 hours or until doubled in size.
4. Make Fillings: In separate bowls, mix together the ingredients for the cream cheese filling and the blueberry filling.
5. Preheat the oven to 375°F (190°C) and line a baking sheet with parchment paper.
6. Roll Out Dough: Roll out the risen dough on a floured surface into a large rectangle.
7. Cut the dough into 8 equal rectangles. Spread a layer of the cream cheese filling on each rectangle, leaving a border around the edges. Spoon a portion of the blueberry filling on top.
8. Fold the dough over the filling, pressing the edges to seal.
9. Bake: Place the assembled pastries on the prepared baking sheet. Bake for 15-18 minutes or until golden brown.
10. While the pastries are baking, whisk together powdered sugar, plant-based milk, and vanilla extract to make the glaze.
11. Once the pastries are out of the oven, drizzle the glaze over the top. Allow them to cool slightly before serving.

Brandy Pear Pie

Yield: 1 pie

Ingredients:

- Vegan pie crust (From recipe earlier in this chapter or a store-bought vegan pie crust)
- 6-7 medium-sized ripe pears, peeled, cored, and sliced
- 1/2 cup (100g) granulated sugar
- 1/4 cup (30g) cornstarch
- 1 teaspoon (5g) ground cinnamon
- 1/4 teaspoon (1g) ground nutmeg
- 2 tablespoons (30ml) brandy
- Zest of one lemon
- 1 tablespoon (15ml) lemon juice
- Topping:
- 2 tablespoons (30g) vegan butter, melted
- 1 tablespoon (15g) granulated sugar
- 1/4 teaspoon (1g) ground cinnamon

Directions:

1. Preheat the oven to 375°F (190°C).
2. Prepare pie crust according to instructions in the recipe earlier in this chapter or use a store-bought pie crust.
3. In a large bowl, combine sliced pears, granulated sugar, cornstarch, ground cinnamon, ground nutmeg, brandy, lemon zest, and lemon juice. Toss until the pears are well coated.
4. Spoon the brandy pear filling into the pie crust.
5. Cut slits in the top crust to allow steam to escape. Mix melted vegan butter, granulated sugar, and ground cinnamon, then brush it over the top crust.
6. Bake in the preheated oven for 45-50 minutes or until the crust is golden brown and the filling is bubbly.
7. Allow the brandy pear pie to cool before slicing and serving.

Gluten-Free Option:

- Substitute all-purpose flour with a gluten-free 1:1 flour blend for the pie crust.
- Ensure that the cornstarch used in the filling is gluten-free.

Made in United States
Troutdale, OR
03/20/2024